"This is an extremely interesting and provocative book, a fresh take on anarchist theory and how it fits with real human life in all its diversity. I've learned things I didn't know. It is especially revealing on areas of spirituality and faith and their intersection with anarchism, including material I've not seen elsewhere. The book is living proof that an anarchist perspective is the beginning of the intellectual and spiritual process of seeing the world clearly."

Jeffrey Tucker, Economist

The Conscious Resistance: Reflections on Anarchy & Spirituality By Derrick Broze & John Vibes

"Mind" Cover Art by S.M. Gibson @TheSMGibson
"Healing" Cover Art by Robbie Allen, www.RobbieAllenArt.com
Edited by Misty Dawn Cook, www.logophileediting.com

The Conscious Resistance:
Reflections on Anarchy & Spirituality

Part 1 - Naming the Path

Part 2 - Anti-Authoritarianism in World Traditions

-Our Journeys -
Acknowledgments

Chapter 1 - What is the Conscious Resistance?

There is a deep struggle in this world that dates back thousands of years and has created an untold amount of suffering. It is a struggle towards freedom and peace taking place while so-called 'civilizations' are ravaged by slavery, genocide and war. Today, many of us live under the illusion that these horrors are a thing of the past or the problems of some far-away land, but they are just as real today as they were in the middle ages. These problems are just as real in America as they are in the rest of the world.

To heal the widespread suffering in this world there are many social and political changes that must take place. The entire structure of our societies must change in order to achieve peace and freedom for all people. While a truly utopian world is likely impossible, a world without systematic and socially acceptable violence would certainly be a paradise compared to what we have now.

To create the social and political changes necessary to end the violence, we must use a different method than those tried in the past. We cannot simply storm the gates of the castle and hang the masters from the highest trees. This will only result in a new master sitting on the same throne, exactly as we have seen throughout history, again and again.

Real change comes from within. In order to stop this cycle of madness, we need an evolution of consciousness. The state and all of its predatory appendages, like the corporate and military industrial complexes, are more than groups of people with weapons who need to be overthrown– they are bad ideas that can be rendered obsolete with the right combination of good ideas.

As the fight for freedom has evolved, so has our understanding of what "*freedom*" actually means.

The desire to understand and pursuit of "*freedom*" has existed for as long as conscious beings have been on this planet. Different cultures throughout history have had their own ideas and visions of how freedom manifests itself.

Throughout this book, we will be careful to define important terms that may have different meanings for different people.

There are two ways to define philosophical terms like *government, country, democracy, capitalism, communism, freedom, slavery*, etc. We can define these terms theoretically, or we can define them according to how they operate in reality.

For example, many people now recognize the word "*propaganda*" as a negative term used to describe psychological manipulation. However, a hundred years ago propaganda was just another word for "*media*". There are many modern words that are largely defined by their theoretical definition, instead of how they operate in reality. When we define terms throughout this book, we will not only be looking at the standard dictionary definition, but we will also break down what that word has truly represented throughout history.

With "*freedom*" being the very basis of this conversation, it is important to be clear about how we are defining the term.

Freedom is defined by Webster's dictionary as follows:
"*: the quality or state of being free: as*

a : the absence of necessity, coercion, or constraint in choice or action b : liberation from slavery or restraint or from the power of another

: INDEPENDENCE

c : the quality or state of being exempt or released usually from something onerous <freedom from care>"

Pay attention to the first definition of "*free*" - "*the absence of necessity, coercion, or constraint in choice or action*". It is this definition on which we base our vision of freedom. Not only do we advocate a voluntary society free of coercion, but we also advocate that each individual have the utmost control over his or her own life and affairs. Despite the commonly-held belief that humanity would regress to a barbaric state without government, we propose that the individual who

5

governs himself is better equipped to create a free and enjoyable life.

From this definition of freedom we can begin to analyze the history of humanity and decide whether we are living in a state of relative freedom, or in varying levels of slavery. By studying philosophy, economics, politics and history we can determine whether humankind is freer than it was in the past, or if we have been slowly losing our freedom over time.

In the following pages we propose that it is not only humanity's physical struggles for freedom that should be studied, but also our daily internal struggle for freedom. We believe there is a vastly deeper and extremely personal "*fight*" for freedom taking place in every moment. This is the internal struggle, the mental battle, the war waged between our desire for our "highest good" and our doubt and self-imposed limitations, perpetuated by our own internal tyrants. It is on this field where humanity's greatest war is fought.

As a result of our research and experience we have come to conclusion that it is extremely important and necessary to challenge and expose the physical manifestations of power. Equally important is our ability to face and challenge our doubts, fears, insecurities and pain.

No matter how hard and long humans try to establish a freer world, we are doomed to repeat the same mistakes if we cannot conquer our own inner demons. Poverty, corrupt governments and wars are manifestations of our inner struggles, and the fact that we allow these travesties to carry on shows that we are a species in need of deep healing. Until that healing takes place, humanity will be ripe for control by an external source or "*leader*", and in fact, people will be begging for that control.

It is with this thought in mind that The Conscious Resistance was born.

"*Consciously resisting*" means being willing to engage in self-reflection. Without knowing our own doubts, hopes, fears, dreams, insecurities and strengths we cannot truly know what freedom means to us as individuals. Becoming conscious of your actions is one of the most important steps towards understanding and claiming your own freedom

From that clear state of mind one can lead by example and help others in their own pursuit of self-discovery and freedom.

This book is aimed at those who already possess some level of understanding about the search for freedom, but are ready to challenge long-held beliefs about where freedom begins and ends. These essays are for those who live as free humans in the physical realm but desire a deeper, fuller experience of liberty. The words are also written for the spiritually curious; the researcher; the wayfarer who values themselves spiritually but may have yet to consider how to achieve freedom, or may be intimidated by some of the darker aspects of our five-sense reality that need to be overcome.

We would also like to make it clear that this book is not meant to be the final word on ANY of the topics discussed. Rather, we hope to broach the conversation and spark healthy debate about how far one should take their desire for freedom. None of the ideas expressed should be taken as arguments for a monopoly or *"one size fits all"* model of freedom.

In the New Libertarian Manifesto, Samuel E. Konkin III, founder of Agorism, writes:

"There is no One Way, one straight line graph to Liberty, to be sure. But there is a family of graphs, a Space filled with lines, which will take the libertarian to his goal of the free society, and that Space can be described."

We believe The Conscious Resistance, the coupling of self-governance with a sense of self-reflection, is the best path towards the goal of a free society.

Chapter 2 - Explorative Agnosticism

Modern culture is defined by the experience of the five-sense world. Experiences that we can physically quantify and measure set the parameters of reality. Without a doubt, there are phenomena that can be observed and proven with the five senses and there are concepts in this world that are objective. Still, this does not necessarily mean that everyone shares one uniform consensus reality.

There is a vast world beyond our five senses. Despite a lack of understanding of what this world beyond the five senses is composed of, there is a mountain of evidence that proves it exists. It is best for everyone to personally interpret what lies beyond the five senses and respect the interpretations of others, instead of fighting over something that will not likely be proven in our lifetime.

When pursuing a spiritual path, even if an individual's intuition isn't "*real*" or "*true*" in the quantifiable sense, the experience they are having and the information they bring back from their journey, even if it is simply a journey into the deepest reaches of their own mind, can still provide value and facilitate positive growth in this world.

That being said, it seems that the most logical spiritual path to take would be an agnostic one. Before we go forward, it is important to define some of these terms, especially "*spirituality*" and "*agnosticism*."

Spirituality can be defined as:

"An individual's personal set of beliefs about the great mysteries of life and the world beyond the five senses."

Traditionally, the idea of spirituality has been attached to the concept of religion. However, "*Spirituality*" and "*Religion*" actually represent two entirely different philosophies. A religion is a one-size-fits-all-worldview with a hierarchy, a set of rules and oftentimes, a priest class to enforce it all. Spirituality is a free and personal interpretation or connection with a spirit realm or higher power or whatever that person wants to call it. Spirituality is a practice that brings an individual closer to their essence, where essence means a set of attributes that make an object "what it is". To use a comparison, Anarchy is to Statism, as Spirituality is to Religion. Anarchy is the physical manifestation of freedom and spirituality is a mental manifestation of freedom. In contrast, Statism is control in the physical sense, and religion is control in the mental or spiritual sense.

The organized religions of the world have created untold suffering and manipulate wars around the world. They have spread propaganda, instigated genocide, and justified slavery. These facts cannot be ignored. However, that does not mean that these institutions have nothing to teach us. All of the world's religious teachings, from those that border on historical fact to those that are obviously myths, contain a wealth of knowledge that should be considered.

As Aristotle said, *"It is the mark of an educated mind to be able to entertain a thought without accepting it."*

Different cultures have different belief structures based on the lessons taught in their particular region of the Earth. Yet every religion tells essentially the same story, using different words to accommodate whichever culture the tale is coming from.

In the following chapters, we delve into the history of specific religions and their root in anti-authoritarian teachings. We are not advocating these religions, nor are we excusing the political organizations that represent them. We also do not seek to judge anyone who participates in these religions. In fact, we hope to communicate that many religions are rooted in the same spirit of anti-authoritarianism and can coexist peacefully.

We hold the perspective that religious organizations have taken legitimate ancient spiritual teachings and corrupted them with their own political ideologies. This is why many religions seem to have the same basic truths, but also much of the same poison and disinformation. A positive spiritual philosophy usually turns into a violent control mechanism when it is corrupted by a figure of authority. It is at this point when everything changes– the goals are no longer to discover powerful truths, but to fear the future and cling to the past in order to serve some master.

At our current stage of evolution we have about the same chance of understanding the spirit realm as a goldfish has of understanding quantum physics, so it's absolutely insane for us to be killing each other in the name of god. At the heart of this ignorance is fear– fear that has been stirred up and manipulated by our oppressors for many generations. They have preyed upon our natural fears of the unknown, of change, and of death, while only giving us fractions of information about our existence.

We can now look back throughout history and see that most wars and crusades in the name of religion were actually wars over land, resources and empire expansion. The rulers of the time used their subjects' deep fear of god to manipulate them into going on crusades, just as our rulers today use fear tactics to con us into fighting and dying in wars. Like pawns on a chessboard, men and women are sent out to war by an almighty authority, who believes they are expendable. This kind of senseless carnage is still taking place without much questioning from the public. Insignificant differences among common people of all nations are still used by those in power for the sake of conquest. Whether those differences are religion, race, economic status or culture, they are used as justifications to commit atrocities.

Technically speaking, Agnosticism is the perspective that supernatural matters cannot be proven or disproven. Agnosticism is traditionally defined as:

the view that any ultimate reality (as God) is unknown and probably unknowable; broadly

: one who is not committed to believing in either the existence or the nonexistence of God or a god

Historically, agnostics have chosen to stay away from supernatural topics altogether. The position advocated in this book takes a more hands-on approach. We believe there is wisdom and self-discovery to be gained from seeking to understand and participate in the world beyond the five senses.

Explorative Agnosticism is strongly different from atheism because there is no claim of truth beyond the five senses and there is no expectation as to what other people believe. While atheism claims to be a non-religion, some of its loudest advocates seem as concerned with evangelism as born-again Christians. Militant atheists are very intent on changing people's minds about whether anything lies beyond the five senses and will often form their opinions of others based on whether they believe in a higher power. The same can be said of fundamentalists of any faith and this, of course, does not apply to all atheists. A fundamentalist of any religion will claim that their perception is superior, so this is surely a view held by some atheists.

Agnostics, on the other hand, feel that it doesn't really matter what people believe about anything that goes on beyond the five senses because none of it can be proven. There is no expectation of what others should believe and there is no personal investment in philosophical conversations. While mainstream religions and even modern atheist philosophies rely on the masses for validation, agnostics' personal connection with nature, the universe or god(s) is validated only by their own intuition, and doesn't depend upon the approval of others. Following that same standard, there is no need to take a role in validating or judging others, as long as they commit no physical transgressions. Agnostic-atheists may have their own atheistic beliefs, but also understand that their beliefs are just as fallible as an ancient myth.

We find agnosticism to be the most logical position to hold. However, this does not mean that the realm of the supernatural is not worth exploring.

This is why the term *"Explorative Agnosticism"* is so important to this discussion. While supernatural phenomena cannot be measured or proven, exploration of these realms is a worthwhile quest and necessary for the advancement of our species on this planet.

Of course, we cannot define what supernatural realms look or feel like, or how an individual should interpret them. We are simply advocating an open-minded approach to the information presented in this book. While we understand and value rational thinking and logic, we also understand that sometimes humans are better served by intuition and imagination. In fact, humans are best served when there is a balance of these two polarities.

It is in the world of imagination, creation, self-reflection and deep connection to the non-physical that rational thinking often proves insufficient. You might experience a transcendental state of meditation leading to insight about your path, but the rational side of your brain may tell you to disregard gnosis gained from such states of *"incoherence."*

Perhaps you participate in a sweat lodge and drumming ceremony and find yourself carried away on a cloud to a distant location to communicate with animal spirits. Logic may tell you to disregard these experiences as nothing more than irrelevant dreams or outright fabrications.

We, however, believe it is not up to the collective to decide what is *"real"* and valuable for another person in their experience on their path.

To illustrate this, we like to imagine four individuals standing in a meadow witnessing the scene from four different perspectives. We could call these perspectives the Objective, Subjective Symbolic, and Holistic.

In the Objective world, you might notice the physical aspects of the scene. The colors of the plants, soil and sky, the square footage, the variety of plant life and so on. In this world, the fundamental belief or assumption is that Everything is Separate.

From the Subjective world, one may have an understanding of the interdependence of the natural world and the mutually supportive roles played by all it's elements and creatures. This Subjective world is a deeper experience than the Objective world, where you may be able to commune with plants and animals. The fundamental assumption in this world is that Everything is Connected.

Looking from the meadow of Symbolic perspective, you are now seeing nature as a representation of yourself. The open meadow is your openness to life and you may feel called to express yourself artistically with this symbolic perspective. You come to know that everything is a part of a pattern and exists in relationship to something else, and that everything means what you decide it means. In this world you know that Everything is Symbolic.

From the Holistic world, you have transcended from standing in front of the meadow and observing it to becoming one with the meadow. Now the sunlight is shining on you leaves and being turned into your energy. The bees are gathering your pollen as you experience the moment as a flower. You feel the sensation of drinking the nectar as the bee. The fundamental assumption in this realm is that Everything is One.

In our view, every individual experience is valid, regardless of the world which it takes place. Further, what rings true and factual in the Objective World will not be so for those experiencing life from one of the other realms.

Someone stuck in a strictly rational, materialist, reductionist mindset will not understand the reality experienced by someone operating in a more intuitive state.

Lastly, it's important to remember that the biggest obstacle to successfully moving between these worlds (and thus improving our ability to communicate with a wide range of people) is interference of critical analysis from other levels.

This is the frontal lobe, the analytical part of you that is difficult to quiet during meditation. This is the part of you that will likely doubt the legitimacy of self-reflection and might tell you "this silly hippy stuff isn't going to do anything for you! You should stop reading now!"

In order to gain a better understanding of ourselves, our world and what it means to be a free human being, we must practice removing our assumptions and doubts. King recommends remembering this when moving between worlds, weather physical or ethereal. From this standpoint we believe Exploitative Agnosticism to be a beneficial position.

As free people, our beliefs about the world should not be limited or controlled by the collective.

And as such we do not care if others doubt or deny our beliefs because we make no effort to doubt or demean their beliefs about the spiritual, non-physical world. Quite simply, our interpretations of the world beyond the five senses are not dependent on any one person, institution, or book.

If we are to know ourselves as spiritually liberated beings we must open our hearts and minds to the possibilities that wait outside the quantifiable world.

Chapter 3 - Reality Beyond the 5 Senses: Beyond Logic, Beyond Reason

The religion of Materialism is the dogma that rules modern popular culture and the realm of mainstream science. The Materialist believes only that which we can see, touch, smell, taste, feel and measure quantifies reality. The materialist also believes that any discussion of what lies beyond the five senses is foolish and not worth consideration. This worldview is shaped by the unproven assumptions of mainstream science, which is important not to confuse with the scientific method.

The scientific method describes a process of experimentation in which theories are tested and either proven or disproven. This is a great concept that helps us to better understand the five-sense world of matter, but the political establishment that we know today as mainstream science is no longer rooted in the scientific method. Instead it has become like a new religion. However, there is a blind spot in this point of view. Much to the dismay of materialists, science has many times helped humans unveil the world of superstition.

Many of the experiments carried out today in government labs begin with their conclusions pre-planned and many topics are entirely off-limits for scientists to explore. For example, it is taboo for an archeologist or anthropologist to present an alternative view of history with their scientific findings. Scientists have dismissed researchers like John Anthony West and Graham Hancock, who presented evidence that the mainstream view of Egyptian history was entirely misdated and incorrect.

These researchers had significant evidence that many structures in Egypt date back much farther than scientists initially projected. Mainstream science dates the construction of the Sphinx to around 10,000 years ago, while West and Hancock proved that certain significant weathering on the structure must have occurred at least 30,000 years ago. Despite this groundbreaking discovery, their evidence was rejected by mainstream science because it didn't fit in with official narrative.

Another rebel who has been challenging the unproven assumptions of materialism is scientist Rupert Sheldrake. Sheldrake courageously conducts his own independent experiments, based in the scientific method, which set out to explore areas that are too *"weird"* or taboo for mainstream science to take seriously.

One of Sheldrake's experiments provided compelling evidence that many pet owners have a telepathic connection with their animals. In the experiment, dogs were observed waiting for their owners to come home. Every dog would become excited moments before they received any physical indication that their owner was nearby. Sheldrake would have the owners take different ways home at different times of the day, drive different cars, take the bus, walk, wear different shoes, an unfamiliar aftershave or perfume, etc. This ruled out the possibility that the dogs were simply using their heightened sense of smell or hearing. Regardless of how the experiment was framed, the animals were always able to sense when their owners were coming home. While this does not definitively prove a telepathic connection, it does show a strong correlation between humans and animals, which suggests that this is a point of view at least worth considering.

Sheldrake also assembled some compelling evidence for the case of crop circles. In a brilliant experiment, Sheldrake hoped to gauge how talented human crop circle artists actually were. If it were possible to see the best job a human could do with a crop circle, then it would be much easier to deduce whether other random crop circles had been created by a human hand or some other technology. To get to the bottom of this question, Sheldrake hosted a contest with a massive cash prize for the best crop circle and participants entered from around the world. Though they created incredibly elaborate crop circles, they were still not as elaborate as others that have been recorded in countrysides around the world.

Another field we feel the scientific establishment needs to catch up with is the idea of reincarnation, or remembrance of past life experiences. Traditional thought says that when a human body expires so does conscious experience. However, there is abundant evidence indicating that children are sometimes born with memories of formerly-lived lives.

Take, for example, the story of James Leininger. James is the focus of the book Soul Survivor: The Reincarnation of a World War 2 Fighter Pilot. The book discusses how Leininger began having nightmares, recalling violent scenes of planes being shot down and ensuing death. He was only two years old when these nightmares began. Leininger's parents say he would draw very detailed pictures of battle scenes complete with fighter jets from America and an enemy that seemed to be Japanese.

James' parents began searching for clues as to what their son was speaking about and whether or not he was experiencing some type of mental delusion. The two-year-old child exhibited an uncommon knowledge of the mechanics of World War 2 planes and would even detail memories of what he said was a past life as James, WW2 fighter pilot.

After researching some of James's claims, his parents were able to confirm the names of several people he said he had fought alongside. Eventually the family learned that James Leininger somehow had detailed memories of James Huston, a fighter pilot who crashed into the ocean near Iwo Jima after being fired upon by the Japanese. When asked for specifics about his memories, the young child was able to identify his ship as the Natoma. James Leininger also correctly identified the name of Jack Larsen, a friend of Huston's and the pilot who was flying next to Huston when he was shot down.

Upon meeting veterans of the USS Natoma Bay, James Leininger was able to recite specific names and places from the war. The Leininger family went even further and made contact with the family of James Huston. James met the sister of James Huston and told a story of a painting done by Huston's mother. This painting had not been seen by anyone other than the Huston's deceased mother and the siblings. Huston's remaining family was amazed at the detail the young boy was able to recall nearly 60 years after James Huston had died.

Jim Tucker, professor of psychiatry and neurobehavioral sciences at the University of Virginia, has studied over 2,500 cases of children who report memories of past lives. In a January 2014 interview with National Public Radio, Tucker describes the difficulty in fitting these phenomena into a strictly materialist worldview…

"I think it's very difficult to just map these cases onto a materialist understanding of reality. I mean, if physical matter, if the physical world

is all there is, then I don't know how you can accept these cases and believe in them. But I think there are good reasons to think that consciousness can be considered a separate entity from physical reality."

Tucker references Max Planck, the father of quantum theory. Planck believed consciousness was fundamental and that matter was derived from it. This could indicate that consciousness and superconsciousness, or experiences of extra, are not necessarily dependent on a physical body or brain.

So what exactly is consciousness? Before we delve deeper into expanding on consciousness, we should take a moment to define the word, as we have defined other key terms.

Consciousness is defined as:

:the condition of being conscious : the normal state of being awake and able to understand what is happening around you
:   a person's mind and thoughts
:   knowledge that is shared by a group of people

As we have noted, the mainstream view of science operates from a place of ignorance when it comes to what consciousness is or where it resides. The accepted dogma is: Matter is life and anything beyond the physically measurable world is irrelevant to scientific pursuit. Rather than ignoring or condemning that which is unknown by the scientific community or the rational mind, we believe in remaining open to the endless possibilities.

The topic of consciousness is a highly contentious field. Beyond just what and where consciousness is, there are also questions of animal and plant consciousness that we will explore in more detail later.
One area where spirit, science and history align is the topic of quartz crystals. Quartz crystals are often used in "*New Age*" circles for trading, ceremony and, some believe, healing. Though a rational man may dismiss these trinkets as fantasy, they have both a scientific and historical relevance. There are several types of quartz crystals. These include amethyst, citrine, rose, smoky and clear quartz. The crystals are composed of silicon dioxide molecules and other impurities. Crystals containing only silicon dioxide are known as clear quartz. The atoms within crystals

vibrate at a stable frequency, making them excellent receptors and emitters of electromagnetic waves.

Quartz crystals are piezoelectric, meaning they can turn energy from one form into another when pressure is applied. When mechanical pressure is applied to a quartz crystal, it vibrates, producing a voltage that can be converted from mechanical forces into electrical signals. Quartz crystals have been used in many common items, such as radios, watches, sonar and ultrasonic generators, and hearing aids. They can also be used to make glass, mortar, grindstones, sandpaper and cleaning compounds.

One of the first people to recognize the uses of quartz was Nobel prize winner, Marcel Vogel. Vogel was a research scientist for IBM when he discovered that crystals can be programmed as silicon chips in a computer. He came to believe that crystals could be programmed through thought. He wrote that thoughts were a form of energy that can be directed through intentions. Specifically, he created devices that he said allowed users to program their intentions onto a crystal and then transfer them to water. He likened the process to the way an inductor in electronics creates an energy field in components in proximity to the field. Despite, or perhaps because of, his prolific work and extreme foresight, his work was denounced as pseudoscience.

We now know that Quartz has a place in both the modern scientific and mechanical worlds. But scientists and mechanics were not the first to acknowledge the power of crystals. Quartz crystals have been popular for centuries, possibly millennia, with indigenous peoples around the world. Amazonian Shamans and healers communicate with spirits they believe live within the crystals. In his book, *The Cosmic Serpent,* anthropologist Jeremy Narby writes about the use of crystals by indigenous peoples and a possible relation to DNA. Narby discusses how Australian Aborigines believe life was created by *"the Rainbow Snake"*, symbolized by quartz crystals. He also mentions the Desana of the Amazon who believe an anaconda created life and symbolize the creator with a quartz crystal.

Narby goes on to inquire how these varied cultures, separated by time and space, could have possibly come to such similar conclusions. He suggests these cultures may have been aware, from their perspective and understanding, of what modern science and its tools of measurement have yet to discover. Perhaps the spirits communicating with these cultures through the use of hallucinogenic plants and altered states of mind was a form of direct communication with DNA, what Narby calls the Cosmic Serpent.

DNA itself has a historical connection to crystals. Erwin Schrödinger was the first physicist to propose the idea of an aperiodic crystal containing genetic information. DNA had already been discovered, but its helical structure and role in reproduction had not. Schrödinger proposed the existence of a hereditary material responsible for all life. He called this an aperiodic crystal, which unlike a standard crystal, does not repeat itself and can produce an infinite number of possibilities with limited atoms.

These examples offer starkly different viewpoints on what crystals and DNA are and what purpose they serve. Different cultures and researchers from vastly different backgrounds, using tools both modern and archaic, physical and intuitive, arrive at similar conclusions. They are unable to recognize the similarity of their discoveries due to an experiential barrier. The information could be identical yet the presentation and reception of the information are dependent on the one receiving said information.

As Narby noticed while living amongst and studying indigenous peoples, the objective mind often cannot rationalize or fathom that which has not yet been uncovered. He spoke of the importance of defocalizing the gaze, and specifically, he learned to take the word of the natives he worked with, regardless if what they said made objective sense. He spoke of *"objectifying one's own objectifying relationship"*, or to *"become aware of one's own gaze."* We should remember this valuable lesson as we consider information that may be beyond our current understanding or comprehension.

Chapter 4 - Towards Panarchy: Anarchy Without Adjectives

Since "*Anarchy*" is one of the most maligned and misunderstood words in the English language, we are going to use a very simple definition that gets straight to the point for the purposes of this conversation. Simply put, Anarchy is a social arrangement in which there are no "*rulers.*" A ruler is defined as a person who claims unwanted authority over another life. Sadly, there cannot be a master without a slave, and by the nature of the relationship, the slave is physically and morally obligated to obey the commands of the master. Many people believe this relationship is the stitch that holds the fabric of civilized society together, while in reality, nothing has caused more pain and suffering in this world than corrupt authority and the concept of rulers and slaves.

These social relationships are the manifestations of the internal struggles that exist within us. The relationships between rulers and slaves, kings and subjects and even presidents and citizens do not exist in reality. They are mental constructs, which allow some people to harm and take advantage of others in the open while maintaining moral superiority. This is far more dangerous than the relationship of a common criminal to his victims. When someone attacks from a position of authority, with moral justification, his crimes will go unpunished, and his power will be amplified as a result. This is why police brutality and government corruption have been a problem since before ancient Rome. The relationship of authority breeds and encourages corruption.

That being said, to achieve anarchy, or the abolition of masters and slaves, the solution is far more complicated than simply having a revolution and taking on the current establishment in physical combat, though some argue that this will be a part of the process. This has been attempted many times before and each time power has shifted hands, but the cycle of violence and slavery has continued.

This cycle has been in constant repetition throughout the generations. While power has shifted hands over time, very little has actually changed about how our species views the world, how we view one another, or how we view ourselves as individuals. This is not by mistake. Mountains of propaganda have been released over the centuries to reinforce the old ways and to keep people from thinking outside of the box.

Thankfully, there were a number of brave philosophers who recognized this dynamic and worked to construct a philosophy of anti-authoritarianism, which came to be known as *"Anarchism"*. Later we will explore the anarchist themed writings of Lao-Tzu, from back in the 6th century. There are those who believe Christ was the first Anarchist. William Godwin, a writer in France during the 1790's, is said to have been the first philosophical anarchist with his book *Political Justice*. The first person to publicly proclaim himself an Anarchist was Pierre-Joseph Proudhon, with the publication of his seminal work *What is Property?* in 1840.

Around that time in America, Anarchism was taking roots in the abolition movement. Many abolitionists recognized that slavery and government were essentially the same thing and that slavery will exist in one form or another as long as government exists. One of the main pioneers in American anarchist thought was outspoken entrepreneur and abolitionist, Lysander Spooner. Unlike many other anarchist philosophers in Europe, Spooner's breed of anarchism was strictly individualistic, with a strong emphasis on markets and property rights. Spooner was also very critical of collectivist ideas like democracy and constitutionalism, so his work was heavily focused on deconstructing these concepts and showing them as deceptive forms of oppression.

Spooner thought of a way to put his philosophy into action by creating his own businesses that would directly compete with government services. One of his most groundbreaking entrepreneurial achievements was forming the *"American Letter Company"*, a letter and package delivery business that competed with the US Postal Service and proved that we don't need the government to deliver mail. Hundreds of years later this strategy was identified by Samuel Edward Konkin III as *"Agorism,"* a philosophy of non-compliance that uses underground markets as a means of making the state obsolete. We will be exploring the potential of Agorism throughout this book.

As with many other popular schools of thought, anarchism has evolved and even splintered off over the years in various directions, creating a number of sub-sects within the philosophy. In the 1870's, Europe saw a great divide between anarcho-communists and anarcho-collectivists.

Around the same time, American anarchists were debating the pros and cons of individualist and communist-anarchist thought. As a result, anarchist philosophers in Europe and America began calling for "anarchism without adjectives", which was essentially an acceptance of all those who believe in self-governance and a lack of coercion regardless of their particular economic solution.

Most recently, libertarian activist and writer Karl Hess discussed the need for what he called "*Anarchism Without Hyphens.*" Hess was well-known for working in and out of political circles, with Anarchists on the left and the right. In 1980 he outlined his argument for Anarchy Without Hyphens.

"There is only one kind of anarchist. Not two. Just one. An anarchist, the only kind, as defined by the long tradition and literature of the position itself, is a person in opposition to authority imposed through the hierarchical power of the state. The only expansion of this that seems to me to be reasonable is to say that an anarchist stands in opposition to any imposed authority.

An anarchist is a voluntarist.

Now, beyond that, anarchists also are people and, as such, contain the billion-faceted varieties of human reference. Some are anarchists who march, voluntarily, to the Cross of Christ. Some are anarchists who flock, voluntarily, to the communities of beloved, inspirational father figures. Some are anarchists who seek to establish the syndics of voluntary industrial production. Some are anarchists who voluntarily seek to establish the rural production of the kibbutzim. Some are anarchists who, voluntarily, seek to disestablish everything including their own association with other people, the hermits. Some are anarchists who deal, voluntarily, only in gold, will never co-operate, and swirl their capes. Some are anarchists who, voluntarily, worship the sun and its energy, build domes, eat only vegetables, and play the dulcimer. Some are anarchists who worship the power of algorithms, play strange games, and infiltrate strange temples. Some are anarchists who only see the stars. Some are anarchists who only see the mud.

They spring from a single seed, no matter the flowering of their ideas. The seed is liberty. And that is all it is. It is not a socialist seed. It is not a capitalist seed. It is not a mystical seed. It is not a determinist seed. It is simply a statement. We can be free. After that it's all choice and chance.

Anarchism, liberty, does not tell you a thing about how free people will behave or what arrangements they will make. It simply says that people have the capacity to make arrangements.

Anarchism is not normative. It does not say how to be free. It says only that freedom, liberty, can exist."

We understand that because of its anti-capitalist roots, many Anarchist thinkers on the left might say that Anarchism without Adjectives or Hyphens remains anti-capitalist and thus schools of thought like anarcho-capitalism should be excluded. On the other hand, there are many market anarchists and anarcho-capitalists that point to the coercion that is inherent in democracy and socialism, showing that these ideas are essentially nothing more than government. In short, there is a great deal of debate about who is a "real anarchist" and who isn't among anarcho-capitalists and anarcho-communists.

There is truth to both of these viewpoints. Although market activity is peaceful and voluntary, the social system that has traditionally been called *"capitalism"* is far from a free and voluntary market. Capitalism has used state power as its primary mechanism of operation, so it is not fair to associate this term with a free and open market. Likewise, most traditional democratic and socialist societies have been ruled by a very few rich people, despite the notion that these philosophies are exercised for and by the common people. Even the more egalitarian democratic societies sometimes fall victim to the tyranny of the majority and citizens are forced to live at the whim of their neighbors and change their lives because a vote was held somewhere.

Capitalism, communism and socialism are all loaded terms that have so many different definitions to different people that they are nearly impossible to communicate about. There is no hope in "saving" or "reclaiming" any of these words. They have been tainted by state influence for generations, searing their assumed definitions into the minds of billions of people.

In advocating for an entirely new and different way of life, using the names of old social systems and old ways of doing things seems counterproductive. Of course, there is value in bringing the old terms into the conversation for the sake of comparison, but social philosophies by the names of capitalism and socialism have been around for centuries, and have been government-based economic systems.

For us, the definition given by Kevin Carson, author of *The Iron Fist of the Invisible Hand Corporate Capitalism as a State Guaranteed System of Privilege*, best defines the rise of Capitalism over the centuries

"...industrial capitalism, to the same extent as manorialism or slavery, was founded on force. Like its predecessors, (crony) capitalism could not have survived at any point in its history without state intervention. Coercive state measures at every step have denied workers access to capital, forced them to sell their labor in a buyer's market, and protected the centers of economic power from the dangers of the free market. To quote Benjamin Tucker again, landlords and capitalists cannot extract surplus value from labor without help of the state. The modern worker, like the slave or the serf, is the victim of ongoing robbery; he works in an enterprise built from past stolen labor."

In that sense we are against crony-capitalism, or the subsidizing and protection of business interactions by the state. This is, of course, because states require force and theft to maintain control. On the other hand we are also against involuntary democracy and forced socialism, where people are forced into associations with others because they happen to share the same geography.

Many pioneers of the Anarcho-Capitalist philosophy have made strong arguments for the importance and morality of markets, property and trade, bringing a new perspective to the growing culture of Anarchism. Economist Murray Rothbard coined the term *"Anarcho-Capitalism"* in 1949 or 1950.

Rothbard's writing on banking, property rights and the history of war was groundbreaking and highly academic, but he did not have the same knack for public relations and marketing as he did for economics and history.

Rothbard had some incredible ideas, but he took the two most hated words in the English language and put them together, which sometimes makes a philosophy a hard sell. Rothbard also made several strategic mistakes throughout his career, namely teaming up with politicians and Washington lobbyists in hopes of changing the system from the inside.

Rothbard's work was built primarily upon the work of Ludwig Von Mises, the founder of what came to be known as the Austrian School of Economics. Mises was not explicitly an anarchist and he too had no problem forming alliances with aristocrats and politicians. However, the work he did throughout his life explained exactly how market activity could make the state obsolete. Rothbard later applied these ideas to his anarchist philosophy.

Today, there are anarcho-capitalist economists of all varieties devoting years of research towards developing stateless solutions and voluntary ways to provide goods, services and charity. Meanwhile, there are many mutualists and anarcho-syndicalists who are working to tackle some of the pre-existing state influences that create widespread inequality in our world and finding ways to run worker owned cooperatives.

The subject of property is one of the most contentious topics among anarchists of different varieties. We feel that there is something to learn when considering each side of this debate.

Anarchists who oppose the concept of owning property often point to the government enforcement of property titles and the huge disparity of land ownership in the world and argue that property is a tool of oppression.

They make valid points about how there is a need to reconsider how to deal with property in a free society, but they do not adequately make the case for ruling out property as a concept altogether.

In today's economic atmosphere, property rights have a somewhat negative stigma, due to the offensive amount of government-protected land and resources that have been acquired through force, theft, fraud and coercion. This is an understandable objection, but since the property was illegitimately acquired, it should legally be considered stolen property. The insane amount of land that is unjustly owned by the royal families and governments of the world creates the illusion of scarcity of land, where there is actually abundance. It is virtually impossible for such small groups of people to control and maintain such large areas of land unless they have a legal monopoly on the use of force.

The problems in wealth disparity that we see today do not indicate a problem with property rights. They indicate that property rights have been systematically abused. The fact that the aristocracy unjustly controls this land today shows that mass reparations and restitution are in order. This is no case for the abolishment of property rights, but it is often used as such. Just because the government has monopolized the currency and centralized the trading structure does not mean that economics is a construct of government. Quite the opposite is true– the economy functions very much in spite of government. We would be able to create a world of abundance if it weren't for governments intervening to prop up affiliated businesses and stomp out competition.

The concept of homesteading is the one area of common ground between anarchists who disagree on the subject of property. According to direct homesteading, property belongs to whoever is living in, or making use of a particular piece of land or property. If homesteading had been applied to slave plantations in colonial America, the slaves would technically be considered part owners of the plantation, or each would own an individual piece of the plantation, because they were the ones physically living and working on the land.

Claiming large areas of land by planting flags or drawing lines on a map is not a legitimate way to homestead property. This is a very important concept because it keeps illegitimate landlords from using property as a tool of oppression.

Despite the many differences between the various anarchist philosophies, there is actually a lot of common ground to explore, if each side would only engage in polite conversations on the issues at hand. For example, a great opportunity exists in studying the similarities between the philosophies of Agorism and Mutualism.

Mutualism is the school of thought that seeks to give individuals, rather than the state, control over a piece of the means of production. In *The Practicability of Mutualism*, Clarence Lee Swartz writes, "*Mutualism is a social system based on reciprocal and non-invasive relations among free individuals. The Mutualist standards are:*

-         *Individual: Equal Freedom for each - without invasion of others*

-         *Economic: Untrammeled reciprocity, freedom of exchange and contract - without monopoly or privilege*

-         *Social: Complete freedom of voluntary associations - without coercive organization*"

Mutualist economies might manifest as mutual-credit banks, or worker owned cooperative farms.

Agorism is the philosophy of creating alternative institutions to directly compete with the state. Samuel Konkin III called for participation in Counter-Economics, or economic activity that is typically seen as illegal or unregulated by the state. This includes competing currencies, community gardening schemes, tax resistance and operating a business without licenses. Agorism also extends to the creation of alternative education programs, Free Schools or SkillShares, and independent media ventures. Also essential to Agorism is support of entrepreneurs who actively do business outside of the state's license and regulations.

The Agorist-Mutualist alliance represents an opportunity for Anarchists of all stripes to focus on common ground and build institutions that can help us live free now. Both philosophies reject non-defensive violence, politics and monopolies. Both philosophies do not wish to use the force of the state or some "*dictatorship of the proletariat*" to meet their goals. Both philosophies support the experimentation of a variety of communities, working outside the state to create institutions which give our brothers and sisters who remain in the state's grasp another option, outside the corporate-state monopoly.

It is important to note that the idea of creating alternative institutions does not end at the economy. We would do well to support alternative forms of food production, community defense, education, governance, media and open-source technologies as well, all of which give the people a choice that extends outside of the state and weakens its power over time.

There is value in all anti-authoritarian literature and philosophy, though each side of the argument also has plenty of blind spots. That being said, we believe in Panarchy, or acceptance of all individual's sovereignty and their possible economic solutions as long as they are absent of force. This would allow for all individuals who claim their right to self-governance and seek the absence of coercion to break free from the state with other free humans with similar goals. We choose to find common ground with other Anarchists to move past the state and then allow for free experimentation of all communities and all economies.

Furthermore, it is important to encourage everyone to accept the idea that people do not need to be forced into associations and relationships with one another because they happen to live in the same area. In some circumstances it may be necessary to migrate to the same area to create a commune or a type of protected community.

However, as long as it is logistically possible for people to arrange themselves peacefully in the same geographical region, they should still be able to subscribe to different views on economics, spirituality or any other controversial topic that divides people politically. The only common thread that need tie communities together is the mutual belief that they have no right to force their beliefs on anyone else.

Voluntaryism is the idea of mutual non-aggression. You may notice us refer to this term throughout the book. On the surface, voluntaryism is just another word for anarchism. However, it denotes some very specific philosophical principles that take the definition of anarchism a step further. A voluntaryist not only believes in a world without rulers and slaves, but also advocates for a society built on a culture of peace, non-aggression and a general *"live and let live"* atmosphere.

The Voluntaryist newsletter has defined the philosophy in the following way:

"Voluntaryists are advocates of non-political, non-violent strategies to achieve a free society. We reject electoral politics, in theory and in practice, as incompatible with libertarian principles. Governments must cloak their actions in an aura of moral legitimacy in order to sustain their power, and political methods invariably strengthen that legitimacy. Voluntaryists seek instead to delegitimize the State through education, and we advocate withdrawal of the cooperation and tacit consent on which State power ultimately depends."

When exposed to this philosophy for the first time, people often ask for "proof" of its validity. We are conditioned to having our worldview crafted by sacred tomes written by long-dead authority or hero figures. This is not how freedom works. Waiting to be told what to do by a self-interested authority will never lead to a peaceful society.

As we have briefly discussed in this chapter, the philosophy of freedom is a giant web of dissenting viewpoints that have constantly evolved over generations. There is no ultimate authority on what freedom should or will look like. It is important to remember that these are merely a collection of ideas spread by brave individuals who dared to think differently and stand against the slavery of their times.

However, just because there is no "proof" and no official doctrine, the principles of voluntaryism are self-evident in human behavior, human desire, human history, and possibly in the animal kingdom. The vast majority of human beings desire peace. Even the nasty people in the world desire peace for themselves, if not for others. The vast majority of people who want peace and freedom from harm are obligated to allow the same for others. In other words, by placing the expectation of peacefulness on others, you are automatically accepting the obligation not to harm them. Furthermore, if you harm or threaten another person, you are breaking your end of the bargain and forfeiting your own right for peace, allowing them the moral right to use defensive force against your attacks.

These expectations and obligations will of course be broken from time to time, even in a free society. However, the random violence in a free society is manageable on a case-by-case basis, while the systematic violence in today's world, operating under the color of law and false moral superiority, is far more dangerous because it goes unquestioned. Also, when these obligations are broken, the injured or threatened party is morally justified to defend themselves with force if necessary. Various researchers and economists have studied how things are handled when these rules are broken and a number of possible solutions have been suggested. However, these are just predicted solutions, the real solutions will come when millions of minds start working together on these issues and solving problems that stand in their paths. It is through this process of spontaneous order that brilliant solutions will be pulled from the human consciousness.

While the term voluntaryism is only a recent development in the language of freedom, the philosophy that it embodies is age old. As we will explore in later chapters, many of the world's ancient teachings hold this philosophy as their key value.

The Buddha is quoted as saying, *"The wise harm no one. They are masters of their bodies and they go to the boundless country -- beyond sorrow."* In the early teachings of Christianity these ideas came in the form of the golden rule, or *"Do to others as you would have them do to you."* In Islam there is *"La ikrah fi deen,"* or no compulsion in religion. This philosophy runs deeply through many of the world's ancient teachings.

In a region of voluntaryism, Anarcho-Communists, Anarcho-Capitalists, Muslims, Christians and free people of all varieties would live among one another, or within a very close geographical distance, with very few issues. Neither side would imagine they have the moral right to use force or threats against people who did them no harm. In the event that no one could stand each other, they would not hurt one another as long as they still lived according to voluntaryist principles, but would instead freely disassociate and keep to themselves. This possibility is mentioned because a free society would not be a utopia, although it may appear to be when compared to what we see today, because there would be no such thing as morally justified violence except in defense one's own liberty.

The root of the many traumas, pain and suffering that the human family has both inflicted and endured is almost always morally justified violence. Human sacrifice, genocide, torture, arranged marriages and all forms of slavery are examples of morally justified violence, violence that someone in authority either allowed or enforced. If we want to affect long lasting change as freedom seekers, we must challenge the very nature of morally justified violence, instead of analyzing the person on the throne and the policies they make.

Chapter 5 - Tomorrow's Inner Child Will Save the World

With all this talk of freedom and enslavement, it would be shortsighted not to call attention to the abysmal, but improving, relationship between children and adults. There is a great mystery surrounding why adults are often bitter and hostile, even though we raise children like wild beasts to be tamed, or slaves to be controlled. It should come as no surprise that these children eventually become adults who emulate this attitude of domination and spend their lives attempting to tame and control the external world.

The bond between parent and child is one of the strongest human relationships and children have learned valuable life lessons from their families since the beginning of time. Because of this, many authoritarian societies have guided the structure of the family to mold future generations, even before those generations could enter the indoctrination centers that we have come to know as public education. The establishment's most effective form of propaganda is the ability to impose their values on young impressionable children through their parents.

Using the methods of propaganda that exist via the media, education systems and religious institutions, the establishment has created a society where authoritarianism and domination is a part of everyday life. When parents raise their children they draw from a lifetime of propaganda and they feel a great sense of guilt when their child doesn't accept the established norms in society. Children are free and full of spirit. Parents often forget what it's like to be a child and simply don't understand. Their oppressive culture and its abhorrent values have brought them so far away from their spirit that they feel something is wrong if their child does not conform to the establishment's ideals.

This causes parents to be authoritative with their children to encourage conformity. What they are really doing is breaking their children's spirits and preparing them to live in an oppressive world and accept authority. Parents take this aggressive route due to the example that has been set by the established control systems. In our society it is commonplace for authority figures to be controlling and close-minded. Therefore people tend to behave in the same fashion when they fall into a position of authority themselves. Many good people who only want the best for their families put themselves and their children through a lot of pain and turmoil because they believe their child must live a certain way in order to obtain happiness. All of this stress and oppression is often carried out with the best of intentions, but it is with corrupted perceptions that parents are projecting society's ideals onto their children. Today parents aren't passing earthly knowledge and wisdom to their children but instead passing down a long list of cultural assumptions, idiosyncrasies and misconceptions. They are passing along the aggressive, materialistic message of the aristocracy, which has been instilled in them through years of propaganda and indoctrination. Even worse is the fact that these false values are instilled through constant, emotional, sometimes physical, abuse. This has resulted in a situation where many children have been psychologically abused. If almost everyone's childhood is like this, is it any surprise that most of the adults in our society behave in such irrational ways?

As the empire's facade crumbles and the middle class disappears, it is obvious that the ideals of our society are rotten with corruption. It is important that we don't instill the same set of ideals in future generations or we will be doomed to repeat this cycle of dominance and propaganda yet again. We should be protecting our children from the toxic culture that surrounds us instead of forcing them to conform to it. The values that drive our culture are the reason for a great deal of suffering across the world. These values not only have a detrimental personal impact, but also impact other human beings to project the same oppressive, predator energy that is destroying our planet and our species.

For the most part, every generation treats their children with just a little bit more respect then they saw from their parents, especially since the 20th century. Physical child abuse, infanticide and child slavery have been extremely common throughout history. However, in the past century society has become more conscious of the value of human life and those horrors are much less common. Physical child abuse still takes place today, but it is more isolated due to the fear of legal punishment and its recent taboo nature. However, there is still a great deal of emotional and psychological abuse that is dished out to most children, even by the most well-intentioned adults. Children are a minority group who remain second-class citizens in the eyes of most of the world. Their actions are scrutinized, their opinions are ignored and their existence is seen as not much more than a burden. Many adults fear and envy children, even if they don't realize it. This is because the child is a free spirit that represents change, which the adult has been trained to fear. They suppress their fear by attempting to tame and train the child, just as they themselves were tamed and trained.

This "taming" process is extremely confusing and traumatizing for the child, but unfortunately most parents feel that it is their duty to mold their child to obey authority. Not many have questioned the morality or efficiency of this parenting strategy, but it is a question of extreme importance. Our children are the future of this world and if they are not treated with respect and given freedom, then there will never be freedom or respect in our societies. That's not to say that children should be allowed to do whatever they want, but it means that they should not be treated like animals to be trained and controlled.

Our goal here is not to criticize anyone who uses a "mainstream" parenting strategy. Rather, we want to stress the significance of how we treat children and how that is directly related to the kind of adults that we see in our society. There is an old saying that says, *"the hand that rocks the cradle rules the world"*, which is why it is so important to reevaluate how we treat young people. Our children are the future of this world and if they are not treated with respect and given freedom, there will never be freedom or respect in our civilization. In the context of spirituality and social philosophy, it is important to allow a child to choose their own path. Parents can and should teach their children all they know, but at no point should they express disappointment if their children want to explore other social or spiritual philosophies.

Throughout the course of our lives we develop baggage from the various environments that we encounter. We come into this world as pure souls with a clean slate and as we grow we adopt various beliefs and idiosyncrasies from our culture, which eventually manifest as our personal identities. Whether it is race, class, occupation or belief structure, people identify with cultural labels and use those labels to build their personal model of reality.

Children see the natural world with a clearer perspective because their perception is not yet clouded with cultural conventions and other prejudices. This is why concepts like money, time and authority make no sense to children and rightfully so. These are all man-made cultural abstractions. Youth are typically condemned in authoritarian societies because they have not yet been corrupted and molded into obedient, mechanized citizens. If the youth of any oppressive nation were given freedom to grow without being indoctrinated into the cultural control system, the whole system would change radically within a single generation. The establishment's stranglehold on the human race is unnatural, immoral and insane, which is why their ideals are always met with resistance by the youth culture.

The ruling class knows that their only hope of maintaining political dominance is to vilify their citizens until they have been indoctrinated into the system. In other words, until they "grow up". However, the human mind is resilient and many of us are able to slip into adulthood with minimal psychological corruption. This growing portion of society may not be popular, but they are very often the source of the positive progress that has taken place throughout history. Some of the greatest minds to have walked the earth have recognized that the idea of "growing up" and "fitting in" places people in invisible cultural prisons and corrupts their natural personal philosophies.

One of the most brilliant thinkers of the last century, Albert Einstein, was one of these people. Einstein believed that imagination is much more important than knowledge and that *"common sense is the collection of prejudices acquired by age eighteen."* He was well aware of the cultural games being played with people's minds. When he was 16 years old, one of his schoolteachers told him he would never amount to anything because of his rebellious, unorthodox attitude. So he did what any free-thinking revolutionary would do – he dropped out of school and pursued his education on his own. Einstein went on to become one of the greatest scientists of all time and maintained his rebellious attitude throughout his entire life. Einstein was against war, elitism and any kind of authority whatsoever. If it was not for his incredible contributions to science, he might have been considered insane or an enemy of the state by the establishment. When someone makes it out of childhood without being corrupted they are usually called naive and told that their unorthodox point of view isn't welcome in society.

Many creative and rebellious people who are in touch with their inner child typically receive such negative feedback from family and peers that they knowingly submit to a culture which makes no sense to them. This is exactly why you have to be a certain age in order to vote or run for political office. The system makes sure to give people enough time to submit to the established cultural model of reality before they are able to have any impact at all on the direction of the society.

There are many cases where we do have much to learn from our elders and it is true that skills we depend upon for survival have been passed down through the generations. However, when it comes to a government setting cultural norms, we cannot deny the existence of an ulterior motive. That motive is always the same– to maintain control of the population and defend the power of the established institutions, so they endure for the next generation. It is possible to learn and mature without "growing up" and limiting yourself with cultural prejudices. Being responsible, respectful and peaceful is what makes you a mature adult. It has nothing to do with fitting in to the established culture.

There is also the importance of imagination, something that tends to have increased potency within the minds of the youth. It is through imagination that we weave our dreams and intentions for the future. A powerful imagination and a relinquishing of fear and doubt can help one experience deep states of meditation and shamanic visioning that remain unavailable to the doubting mind that lacks the imagination needed for creative visualization and, ultimately, manifestation. If we allow our imagination, our thirst for knowledge and our youthful passion to be extinguished, then we allow a piece of ourselves and of the human collective to be forgotten. By recognizing the importance of this passion and taking steps today to cultivate empowering relationships and experiences for future generations, we ensure a more peaceful tomorrow.

Chapter 6 - Consciousness & Rights Applied to Animals, Plants, and Earth

The topic of Consciousness is controversial in the fields of philosophy and science. For hundreds of years the debate has raged on in search of a commonly accepted definition of *"Consciousness"*. The term has been associated with or defined at various times as subjectivity, awareness, sentience, or simply the ability to experience or to feel.

The idea that animals possess some level of sentience, or the ability to feel pain, and express themselves in a way that humans can measure, has proven even more difficult to discuss in mainstream science than human consciousness.

Despite a growing body of evidence that indicates animals have awareness at varying levels, people prefer to deny the possibilities and implications of such an idea. Scientist Victoria Braithwaite wrote a book entitled Do Fish Feel Pain? exploring the topic and offering compelling evidence that fish do indeed feel pain and are sentient beings.

Marc Bekoff, emeritus professor at the University of Colorado, Boulder, is one of the pioneering cognitive ethnologists in the United States. In his paper, *"Aquatic Animals, Cognitive Ethology, and Ethics"*, Bekoff compiled a review of the literature on sentience in fish and other water-dwelling animals. Also, the World Society for the Protection of Animals released a systematic review of the scientific literature on animal sentience. The effort used a list of 174 keywords and the team reviewed more than 2,500 articles. The evidence gathered by Bekoff and the World Society for the Protection of Animals overwhelmingly indicate the existence of conscious action on the part of animals.

The ego-based human perception of animals, especially insects, is that they are emotionless creatures that have no distinct personalities. However, new studies have shown that even cockroaches have unique personalities. In the study *"Group Personality During Collective Decision-Making"*, scientists in Brussels, Belgium, found that cockroaches behave very differently, even when in the same environment, due to their personality. In the study, 304 cockroaches with RFID chips placed on their backs were led through a variety of settings, both light and dark. The scientists measured how quickly the cockroaches were able to find food and shelter. They discovered the cockroaches would all behave differently, even when subject to the same external stimulation.

On July 7, 2012, a prominent international group of cognitive neuroscientists, neuropharmacologists, neurophysiologists, neuroanatomists and computational neuroscientists gathered at The University of Cambridge to assess the conscious experience and related behaviors in human and non-human animals. The statement they wrote is known as The Cambridge Declaration on Consciousness. This international team of scientists stated that, *"Convergent evidence indicates that non-human animals have the neuroanatomical, neurochemical and neurophysiological substrates of conscious states along with the capacity to exhibit intentional behaviors"*.

The evidence consequently indicates that humans are not unique in possessing the neurological substrates that generate consciousness. Non-human animals, including mammals, birds, and many marine creatures, including octopuses, also possess these neurological substrates.

Scientists believe animals communicate and make vocalizations based on physiological effects, such as stress. Recently, researchers at the Wolf Science Center in Austria published a paper called *"Wolf Howling Is Mediated by Relationship Quality Rather Than Underlying Emotional Stress"*, which demonstrated that wolves voluntarily choose their vocal communications, specifically howling and barking. To study the physiological stress response due to social separation, the scientists separated one wolf at a time from the other wolves in their enclosures. The teams collected saliva from the remaining pack mates 20 minutes after removing the first wolf. During this period all the wolves' vocalizations were also recorded.

The wolves would always howl when ever separated. However, the researchers found that the wolves would howl more often for a close friend than for the removed socially dominant wolf. Although the stress was measurable with an increase in salivary cortisol in all cases, the wolves seemed to focus on friendship over social dominance, which indicates some level of cognition and choice, rather than an automatic, inflexible response.

If animals can feel pain, use tools and make choices about how they communicate with one another, is it that difficult to imagine them as aware, complex beings with emotions and thought processes?

In 2014 an Argentine court ruled that Sandra, a 29-year-old Sumatran orangutan, was a "*non-human person*" unlawfully deprived of her freedom and must be freed from the zoo and transferred to a sanctuary. The Association of Officials and Lawyers for Animal Rights (AFADA) argued that Sandra exhibited cognitive functions and deserved the right to a freer life. This marked a huge shift in the treatment of animals in captivity. We look to the future to see how court rulings on animals might redefine the human-animal relationship.

There is a huge disconnect in the modern western world in our diets and our treatment of animals. Many people consume unhealthy animal products that contain antibiotics and other harmful steroids and purchase meat from the Farming-Industrial Complex (aka The Meatrix). In doing so they are supporting the mistreatment of the animals themselves and damage to the environment caused by factory farming. Many people have begun referring to this industry as "*The Animal Holocaust*".

To be clear, we are not asking everyone to become vegetarian or vegan or advocating some form of eco-fascism. Rather, we are asking free individuals to reconsider their level of respect toward the life that surrounds us at all times. We prefer you take an active part in your diet if you choose to be a carnivore. If you have the option, hunt your meal yourself. Spend the time, sweat and energy it takes to claim your meal. At the very least, buy your meat from a local vendor with humane practices that you know or can visit in person. Take the time to give thanks to the life that is passing, the life that will allow you to continue to exist. This is the type of thinking that has permeated indigenous cultures for thousands of years and allowed them to live in relative harmony with the planet.

Whether by growing our own food, hunting animals on our own or simply showing respect to the animals we encounter on a daily basis, we believe cultivating a stronger relationship with the life that surrounds us will strengthen the bonds within our human family and push us closer to a freer, more interconnected planet.

Animals and Humans are not the only conscious beings on this planet, however. Recent studies have found that plants have their own form of communication. Researchers with the University of Western Australia found that corn plants emit and respond to particular sounds. In their study "Towards Understanding Plant Bioacoustics" the team discovered that when plants are played a continuous sound at 220 hz they grow toward the sound. This frequency range is similar to the clicking sound made by the plants themselves. Another study entitled "Plant Communication from Biosemiotic Perspective" reported:

"Plants are sessile, highly sensitive organisms that actively compete for environmental resources both above and below the ground. They assess their surroundings, estimate how much energy they need for particular goals, and then realize the optimum variant. They take measures to control certain environmental resources. They perceive themselves and can distinguish between self and non-self. This capability allows them to protect their territory. They process and evaluate information and then modify their behavior accordingly."

The groundbreaking 2014 study *"Plants Respond to Leaf Vibrations Caused by Insect Herbivore Chewing"*, published in Oecologia by researchers at the University of Missouri, found that the Arabidopsis plant can sense when it is being eaten and secretes an increased amount of mustard oil as a defense mechanism to deter insect attackers. In the study, researchers recorded caterpillar's chewing vibrations and then played them to one group of plants while leaving another group in silence. The plants that could hear the chewing vibrations began releasing the mustard oil.

If we have scientific evidence of plants and animals making rational decisions based on analysis and not simply emotion, perhaps we should re-examine our relationship with the fellow inhabitants of this planet, as well as the planet itself. Groups like the International Tribunal for the Rights of Nature believe that corporations and governments around the world have violated the rights of nature.

The Tribunal and similar groups not only promote the rights of nature, but some believe in a sort of "*Nature Supremacy*", or that the fate of the planet should be put ahead of humanity and, in some extreme cases, that force should be used against humans for the good of the planet. We do not advocate such a position but hope to encourage a debate on how our ideas of a more free world will deal with problems involving the planet and our species.

The pursuit of humanity's co-existence with (or submission to) the Earth has manifested in a wide range of beliefs and opinions on how to interact with the planet and its inhabitants. From one side of the spectrum there is a complete denial of animal or plant consciousness or any possibility of "rights" or mutual-respect. In the middle, we see a healthy level of respect and compassion towards other forms of life– animals, humans, plants and minerals co-existing. On the other extreme side of the spectrum there are those who advocate for a dismantling of all technology and "civilization" (Anarcho-Primitivism), the freeing of animals from research labs and the destruction of such labs (Animal Liberation Front) and the destruction of property and occupying of lands slated for destruction or "development" (Earth Liberation Front).

Another key part of the animal rights issue goes back to property. If an individual believes pets are property they may feel entitled to do as they please with said "property". This could include violent abuse. This individual might claim that someone intervening during the animal abuse has commited a violation of property rights. However, we could also foresee a case where animals are given the same "rights" that are awarded humans with diminished mental capacity. Also, one might conclude that since humans are animals, an attack on another animal is an attack on family, thus justifying intervention. We await further debate.

Many indigenous communities believe that life exists in all forms: plant, stone, human, animal and inanimate forces. We believe the closer we move to respecting all life as equal to our own, the deeper our understanding of liberty becomes. It is not only about pursuing freedom in terms of our individual paths, but recognizing the importance of allowing others to operate under their own freedom of action.

Many of us already speak to our pets as children or companions. Why not acknowledge the life in plants, animals, crystals and the earth that surrounds us?

Chapter 7 - Conscious Healing

We understand it may be difficult to look at the current state of the world and try to imagine the world that we believe is possible. Anarchy and Spiritual Awareness seem far off, considering the unsustainable practices of the world's governments and industries. We do not deny these realities.

We understand that humanity must go through deep personal healing on an individual level before the ills of the world will begin to transform. All the negativity we see manifested in the physical realm is a result of our own internal fears and pains. Once we are ready and willing to face ourselves and begin the healing process we will see an increase in compassion, cooperation and creation.

By choosing to reflect on our doubts, fears, insecurities, hopes and dreams, we can come to know ourselves more deeply and begin to understand the ways we are limiting ourselves. Thus, our knowledge and application of freedom is more full. How can we truly know what freedom means to us as a people if we do not understand ourselves? The truth is we cannot. We may educate ourselves on the failures of the state and maybe even overthrow that state through competition and peaceful resistance, but we will find ourselves facing similar conditions within a couple hundred years or so if we continue to operate on the same level of consciousness. If we do not deal with the root causes of humanity's pain, then we are only applying band aids to a gaping wound that desperately needs healing. Imagine a post-revolution world without a spiritual transformation– educated groups of Anarchists running around battling each other's egos due to lack of empathy and unresolved internal conflict. The revolution without healing is a recipe for disaster. We need to evolve forward– not continue to go in circles.

In light of the need for spiritual healing, we would like to offer several methods that we, through our research and experience, have found extremely valuable. These include techniques that are not typically considered by the strictly rational, materialist individual. As we will discuss later, Shamans and healers of all sorts have long known the potential of the ecstatic transformation created in altered states. Plant medicine, psychedelics, repetitive drumming, flotation tanks and deep states of meditation can all induce altered states. In these altered states we are able to access information that may have been hidden in the recesses of our mind and unavailable to the daily waking mind.

As we explore these paths to self-reflection, note that we are not concerned with proving or disproving any other human experience in the pursuit of healing. Why should we care if someone's wild vision of facing down a demonic representation of his or her pain is real? It does not affect our paths if another free mind describes an experience beyond our current understanding. If the experience is of value to your path and produces healing while respecting the rights of other free humans, then we have no place to condemn your journey. David Nichols, an emeritus professor of pharmacology at Purdue University, elaborates on this point when discussing psychedelic research on terminally ill patients.

"If it gives them peace, if it helps people die peacefully with their friends and family at their side, I don't care if it's real or an illusion."

Indeed, researchers of the effects of psychedelic medicines such as Psilocybin mushrooms, LSD and MDMA (ecstasy), are currently experiencing a renaissance of sorts. Throughout the 1950's and 60's, studies were conducted on alcoholics and terminally ill cancer patients, to study the effects of MDMA on depression. By the 60's, LSD and psychedelics had broken free from the laboratory and entered the mainstream through the counter-culture's free love movement. The human psyche was greatly expanded by the reintroduction of these tools.

As many people know, our species has a long history of using psychedelics for self-healing, meditation and the achievement of enlightening experiences. Our ancestors would take psychoactive substances in group settings, often while playing music and dancing around a campfire. Today's rave culture could be considered a modern form of this type of shamanic activity. While some cultures still carry on these practices the old fashioned way, the western world has manifested shamanic culture in a way that is uniquely fitted to its society. Under the influence of psychoactive substances, our ancestors danced in the woods around a fire playing primitive musical instruments, while we in the present day dance in clubs with flashing lights and loud electronic music. If you think about it, it's really the same idea, just a different generation.

This idea is important in the times we are facing today, because in so many ways the oppressive traditions and culture we have inherited from the dictators of our ancestors are still causing us to act in irrational ways. Psychedelics allow us to think outside the cultural boxes we have spent our lives inside, and often help us recognize the irrational nature of our own actions, allowing us to properly manage and overcome them.

That being said, it's important to remember the big picture when dealing with self-healing and empowerment. We need to share what we learn from the psychedelic experience, with others and use that knowledge to brainstorm workable solutions for the problems going on in the physical world.

While we believe in the potential of the psychedelic experience, we cannot deny the early modern history of the tools and the culture. Therapists were not the only ones interested in these medicines. In fact, the US government spent millions of dollars studying the effects of Psilocybin and LSD. In one of the most famous cases, the government attempted to use LSD as a mind control drug. As part of Project MKUltra, the CIA and the US Army manipulated peoples' states of mind with LSD, hypnosis, sensory deprivation and more. The project was officially exposed in 1975 by a Church Committee investigation of CIA activity within the United States. Other programs such as MKDelta, Project CHATTER, Project BLUEBIRD and Project ARTICHOKE were aimed at mind control and behavior modification. MKULTRA , which was later renamed MKSEARCH, focused on the development of a truth serum for interrogating spies. Many of the documents related to MKULTRA have been declassified. However, Richard Helms, director of the CIA at that time, destroyed the majority of the documents in 1973.

The introduction of psychedelics ripped conservative America from its comfort zone as many people began freely expressing themselves for the first time. However, it is important to point out that the federal government introduced many elements of the 1960's counter culture; Even the celebrated LSD guru and Harvard professor Timothy Leary stated that the CIA was involved in the funding of the dissemination of LSD. It is an incontrovertible fact that the state infiltrates creative movements by attempting to subvert influential leaders in music, arts, politics and philosophy. Agents of the US government who had a hand in the initial release of LSD, Psilocybin and other medicines quickly discovered they could not control them. Whether the funding came from the CIA, the FBI or independent sources doesn't matter. The experience and enlightenment gained through altered states are invaluable regardless of the source of funding over 50 years ago. Earth-shaking revelations provided under the influence of external medicines should not be discarded simply because of the state's attempts to manipulate these beautifully empowering tools.

With the growing acceptance of the use of medicinal Cannabis, psychedelics are experiencing a revival in academic research. In 2006, Roland Griffiths, a psychopharmacologist at Johns Hopkins University School of Medicine, and a team of researchers published an article in the

Journal of Psychopharmacology entitled, *"Psilocybin Can Occasion Mystical-Type Experiences Having Substantial and Sustained Personal Meaning and Spiritual Significance"*. The paper concluded, *"psilocybin occasioned experiences similar to spontaneously occurring mystical experiences."* Two-thirds of those involved in the sessions said they were among the most meaningful experiences of their lives. After that,

Griffith's lab conducted a pilot study examining the possibility of treating nicotine addiction with psilocybin. In this study, the participants had three psilocybin sessions and three cognitive-behavioral therapy sessions to diminish cravings. 80 percent of those who received the psilocybin treatments abstained from nicotine for over six months, while less than 7 percent of those who received traditional nicotine-replacement therapy were successful for more than six months. Those who reported a mystical experience had the most success in breaking their addiction.

Some describe the mystical experience as the ability to step back and view one's life path and decisions as an observer. Imagine a camera pulling back and showing you your life in the grand scheme of existence. Griffiths believes this therapeutic experience leads to long lasting-change in individual behavior following a psychedelic session. Terminally ill patients involved in a New York University study reported a renewed thirst for life as well as less fear of their impending death. Under the right conditions these tools can be guides for healing and transformation.

There is also great danger in not respecting the potential within these medicines. One should be wary of individuals who claim an external substance will lead to everlasting enlightenment. Despite the great opportunity for growth and the fact that the medicines can open *"the doors of perception"* and facilitate deep healing, we should not rely on them as a cure-all. Ultimately the healing must come from a personal decision and the determination to face all that waits within your mind.

The enlightenment gained from these transformative moments is part of the reason the State has condemned psychedelics and those who promote them for so long. As Griffiths notes, *"There is such a sense of authority that comes out of the primary mystical experience that it can be threatening to existing hierarchical structures. We ended up demonizing these compounds. Can you think of another area of science regarded as dangerous and taboo that all research gets shut down for decades? It's unprecedented in modern science,"* (The New Yorker, February 9, 2015, The Trip Treatment).

When it comes to healing from addiction and trauma, Psilocybin is not the only alternative to standard psychotropic drugs. MDMA has also been studied by psychologists for its many potential benefits. In 2012 the Multidisciplinary Association for Psychedelic Studies (MAPS) sponsored a long term study on the benefits of MDMA. As recently as April 2014, researchers with the University Of Connecticut's School Of Pharmacy concluded that MDMA assisted psychotherapy could be useful for treating Post Traumatic Stress Disorder (PTSD).

Also growing in popularity in the modern western world are the medicines Ayahuasca and Ibogaine. Ayahuasca, or yagé, is a medicinal brew made with the Banisteriopsis caapi vine and other plants that contain dimethyltryptamine, or DMT. Shamans of the Amazon have long used the brew to enter into a psychedelic state for deep healing and communion with the spirit world. First introduced to the west in the 1950's, Aya has since inspired a massive tourism industry created around the thirst for a night with the healing medicine.

Although modern Internet educated chemists have learned to synthesize and smoke DMT in the comfort of their homes, the brew is not known as Ayahuasca without the Banisteriopsis caapi vine. Drinking Ayahuasca and smoking DMT produce a similar experience, but are different in intensity and length. Ayahuasca produces an intense trip that lasts several hours and often involves throwing up. Smoking DMT will produce a short trip of around 3-5 minutes with after effects lasting around 20 to 30 minutes.

Studies have found that the human brain produces DMT during dreams, near-death experiences and death. This connection between a random plant medicine in the Amazon and a naturally occurring chemical in the human brain has caused some to believe humans are meant to ingest these medicines. Indeed, when the indigenous peoples of the Amazon were asked where they learned to combine these two random plants from the pharmacy of the rainforest, they said the spirits of the plants themselves instructed them. Both versions of the medicine can produce powerful visions, including contact and conversation with spirits, entities or alien-life forms. No one can say for certain what they will endure, as it is a deeply personal experience, but there are some common threads. Users often report a mystical transformation and renewed vigor for life.

Ibogaine, or Iboga is another plant medicine that is quickly gaining popularity. The Bwiti people of Africa have long ingested the plant for healing ceremonies. With modern medicine, we have been able to isolate Ibogaine from the plant and use it to help treat opiate addiction, depression and PTSD. Per usual, Ibogaine was studied by the governments of the world and then banned, supposedly for having no medicinal use. If you are interested in healing from deep traumas and addictions you must escape the clutches of the State and seek out an Iboga retreat center.

There is also much strength in yoga for spiritual growth and healing. In the study *"Breathing-Based Meditation Decreases Posttraumatic Stress Disorder Symptoms in U.S. Military Veterans"*, University of Wisconsin-Madison researchers found that a practice known as Sudarshan Kriya Yoga can help those with PTSD better manage their symptoms. The idea behind this is that breathing affects the autonomous nervous system, so a consistent breathing practice as seen in yoga can help manage symptoms of PTSD, such as hyperarousal.

Despite the apparent differences in the practices, meditation, yogic breathing and the trance produced through Shamanic exercises seem to create a similar state of mind. Meditation itself is a practice as old as human life. As long as human beings have been conscious we have come to Nature for quiet contemplation and reflection. Over time a great number of meditation practices have been developed, each with its own instructions and insights. While we value and respect these individual methods, we note that nearly any experience can be meditative. There is something to be said for a balanced posture and proper breathing, but a bike ride, a walk under the stars, writing poetry or any practice that offers individual quiet time within your own heart and mind can be considered a form of meditation. The consistent application of bringing one's attention to the present moment is key to any form of meditation. Remaining in the present moment, either through counting breaths, mantras or contemplative thought, allows long-dormant emotions to rise to the surface. From that point an individual can assess how best to deal with the new data.

In the same way that meditation reinforces the endless Now, certain Yogic breathing practices allow an individual to become cognizant of the subtlety that is breathing. Although Yoga is more known in the western world for yogic postures, or asanas, the original intention was a system of healing that involved deep states of mind to protect one from external distraction. Patañjali first recorded the yoga sutras as a guide for those seeking enlightenment and a path towards true liberation. Through meditative practice, physical movement and control of breath, or prana, one can achieve internal peace.

Flotation therapy is an alternative healing method that involves spending time in flotation or isolation tanks. American neuroscientist John C. Lily was the first person to develop what was known at the time as a "*Sensory Deprivation*", or isolation tank. An employee of the US government, Lily developed the first isolation tank in 1954 at the National Institute of Mental Health. He and his colleagues became the first test subjects in their research of the tanks. Eventually the experience came to be known as Restricted Environmental Stimulation Technique (REST).

In float therapy (REST), you are suspended in a dark, bubble-like tank. Earplugs prevent you from hearing much of anything while you float in complete darkness. The tank is filled with 12 inches of salt-water set to a temperature of 93.5 degrees, the temperature of your skin. The matching of temperatures causes you to forget where your body ends and the water begins. A typical float session lasts an hour to an hour and a half. Within that time span, your brain may be racing in worry about what exactly you are supposed to be feeling, or it may remain in thoughts of mundane everyday activity. Typically that goes away after the first ten to fifteen minutes and, as with traditional meditation, you are able to relax more easily with repeated floats.

With no external stimuli to focus on such as light or sound, you are free to float without gravity or restriction of thought. After a period of ten to fifteen minutes you may experience auditory hallucinations, swirling lines or visions, or you may simply find yourself in a deep state of relaxation. This form of meditation has been shown to facilitate great healing and insight.

Military Veterans with are now pursuing float therapy as a way of coping with PTSD. A veteran at an Austin, Texas flotation facility reported, *"[Flotation therapy] allows me to not be distracted by everything else around me and purely focus on what's going on with me,"* (Cody Austell, *"Float therapy helping veterans with PTSD"*). Scientists have studied flotation-REST for a number of years, many concluding that the therapy reduces stress, anxiety and depression while improving sleep quality. For those seeking further study of flotation therapy, we recommend The Book of Floating by Michael Hutchison.

There has also been interest in the potential benefits of gardening therapy treatments for PTSD. Obviously escaping the busy life in the city or the suburbs for a weekend of nature is a common practice for many of us. We yearn to be close to something organic, more connected than manmade structures often allow.

Music also plays a powerful role in facilitating healing experiences. Indigenous cultures that predate modern musical instruments have long understood the power of rhythm. The drumming and shaking of rattles produce the same effect that pulls meditators and yogis into deep trances.

In his essay *"Shamans, Yogis and Bodhisattvas"*, Gary Doore refers to this as *"entrainment,"* or *"the induction of altered states of consciousness by the fixation of attention on a regularly repeating pattern of stimuli."* (Shamans Path, page 217)

When Patañjali writes of Pratyahara he is speaking of removing the effects of external stimuli on the senses. This withdrawal from external stimuli allows one to bring their attention inwards, moment by moment. A meditative practice that focuses on centering one's attention allows for states of entrainment similar to the Shaman and the Yogi. Ultimately, these three practices offer their own unique paths toward healing.

Other powerful tools worth mentioning are Creative Visualization, Positive Affirmation and Manifestation. For some, these words represent the latest fad for the "New Age" crowd or simply the denial of a bleak reality through the repetition of uplifting statements. However, these practices, which seem most effective in conjunction, are a very simple way of creating the reality that you seek. Firstly, creative visualization reinforces the power of imagination and the importance of remaining connected to your inner child. By creating "vision boards" with words and images that represent our desired goals, or by simply meditating on what we would like to see in our lives, we remind ourselves of the steps we must take to achieve those goals. By sitting in quiet reflection and allowing our minds to clear of distraction we can achieve all we desire. Through visualization we can see, smell, taste, hear and touch the ideal situation we are trying to manifest and work through the difficult problems we may be facing.

Once you are comfortable with visualizing your path, it is important to affirm the path. This is where positive affirmation comes into play. Positive affirmation is a highly effective method of programming oneself. We face external programming every day through the corporate media, the government and those we communicate with. One way or another, whether by our own doing or some external force, we will be programmed. The mind is much like a computer that can be loaded with a variety of programs. Many of us buy into cultural and environmental programming that does not empower us as individuals, but rather teaches us to doubt our potential and capabilities. We must take steps to deprogram ourselves from such destructive thinking.

With daily affirmations we can create a positive, compassionate view of ourselves and of the world around us. By using affirming statements such as *"I AM..."* we allow our minds to let go of negative habits and begin to rewrite the pathways our thoughts take. For example– perhaps your insecurities are a constant prison, a paralysis that limits your social life as much as your internal world. By changing your internal self-talk that says you are incapable of certain tasks or that other humans view you in a negative light, and affirming, *"I am capable, I am deserving of love and compassion,"* you can overcome a lifetime of unnecessary insecurities and doubts. Over time this reprogramming of your mind becomes habit. Rather than buying into the limiting thoughts when they appear, you are able to say, *"No, Thank you, I no longer need you!"* and instead tell yourself, *"I am capable, I am loved, I am becoming stronger every day in every way."* This simple act can have long-lasting, life-changing effects. Through creative visualization and daily affirmations, we are not only changing our state of mind and the way we look at our world, but we are energetically altering the course of our lives.

Manifestation is the power of watching an idea go from a seed in your mind, to a daily focus, to a physical reality. Manifestation is the culmination of an empowered individual understanding what they want, making a conscious choice to pursue that goal, calling out to the universe for assistance and taking steps in the physical world to bring that idea into reality. These tools are not simply a method of praying or wishing away the problems we face. We must remember that the power of the mind is assisted by actions taken by the physical body. Through personal responsibility, determination and a focused work ethic we can produce the results we seek and have everything we desire.

As previously mentioned, we are all faced with external programming from a number of sources. Without breaking through that propaganda, the tools we have mentioned will lack their full potential. If you are trying to clear your mind for meditation and all you can think of is how silly you feel, then you won't get very far. If you find your inner voice continuously berating you as you attempt to visualize your way through an emotionally damaging relationship, the likelihood of success is greatly decreased. To combat our internal tyrant we must learn to change our subconscious thoughts. This can be done through consistent application of Conscious Language.

In his book, Conscious Language: The Logos of Now, Robert Tennyson Stevens outlines the power of carefully choosing words that empower, rather than hurt. Stevens explains how it is possible to upgrade the *"Human Operating System"* through words. One method is to catch yourself thinking or speaking limiting thoughts and then transform the words into powerful tools for growth. One example of this is to do away with actions that do not fulfill your highest good. For example, you may always have trouble being punctual and say to yourself, *"I am always late."* With Conscious Language we learn to put those behaviors where they belong - in the past. We then affirm what we want to create in the present moment. Rather than saying, *"I am always late"*, you might try, *"In the past I have been late often, however, in the future, I will be on time."* Maybe you often feel rushed, like you never have time for all of your daily pursuits. Rather than stressing yourself out and focusing on how limited your time is, you should instead affirm, *"I have time and energy for everything I need."*

These are two very simplified examples of using Conscious Language. We encourage each individual to pursue his or her own research of the topic. As with anything, practice makes habit. By learning to speak compassionately and consciously to yourself you can create a more positive and fulfilling physical reality. It is important for our spiritual well-being to create the world we want and express gratitude through our words. In the study *"Gratitude and Depressive Symptoms: the Role of Positive Reframing and Positive Emotion"*, researchers with Brigham Young University confirmed that positive thinking is related to lower signs of depression. As always, you are the master of your reality and experiences.

When maintaining a conscious mind it is also important to maintain a healthy and well-nourished body. Among the average peoples there is a culture of poor eating habits. This is usually the result of ignorance and financial disadvantage, as well as propaganda from state and corporate media. However, since this information has broken through to the mainstream in recent years, there are now a variety of alternative diets being promoted by different researchers. Our intention here is not to tell you how to eat, but rather, to tell you to be conscious about what you eat. Unfortunately, most of the food that is popular and readily available in modern society can hardly be classified as food. The abundance of processed foods has made diligent research necessary when considering your diet.

It is not our job to tell you which path to choose. That is something every individual is free to choose for themselves. It is not free choice and free will that cause problems in this world, it is when individuals are less than conscious about their choices that we see problems manifest.

Chapter 8 - Rites of Vigil and Solitude

This essay features personal anecdotes from Derrick. We offer his experiences as a way of highlighting the role that solitude can play in spiritual growth.

"Nowhere can man find a quieter or more untroubled retreat than in his own soul." – Marcus Aurelius

"No man is free who is not master of himself." –Epictetus

When I contemplate the idea of freedom, the notion that human beings can possess critical thinking skills, a sense of self-determination and compassion for their fellow humans, a number of questions run through my head. What does it take for one to be free? What are the necessities for freedom? In what ways do our unique ideas of freedom differ from one another? In what ways do we create artificial boundaries for ourselves?

We must consider all of these questions to truly understand what freedom means and how to achieve it. While there is not one single road that leads to freedom, our individual experiences provide us with insight that serves as helpful hints, tips and guidance for our brothers and sisters on their individual paths. It is with that in mind that I offer some of my perspective in hope that we may learn from each other.

I would like to focus on the need for occasional solitary sessions, or extended companionless journeys. My experience with solitude has led to deep personal insights and understanding of my doubts, fears and insecurities. The idea behind the conscious resistance is to create a population that encourages self-knowledge, individuality, compassion, awareness and solutions. I believe that until we choose to know ourselves and our motivations and aspirations, we will continue to be ruled over by a small group of people who are not working in the best interest of the whole. In fact, if this "resistance" were to spread, that same small group of people might have a powerful spiritual experience that could lead to an understanding of their place in the whole and a restoration of balance.

Solitary Paths

Twice in my life the universe provided me with opportunities for reflection and meditation, each vastly different from the other. The first involved my incarceration for possession of a controlled substance in 2005. I was less than a month from turning 21 and had been battling addiction to a variety of drugs for the better part of 3 years. At that point the substance that was wreaking havoc in my life was crystal methamphetamine. Despite my current beliefs that people should not be arrested and caged for victimless crimes such as drug use, I now know that my drug use at that particular time was an effort to escape and self-medicate my depression and general lack of understanding of the world.

Upon my arrest and imprisonment I resisted the environment and fought like hell to maintain connection to the "free world". Eventually I had to accept that I was going to spend the next 18 months behind bars. There was not a family member, friend or lawyer who could do anything for me. The only choice was to sit, be with myself and take moments to consider how I found myself in that predicament. I spent the next year and a half writing pages and pages of notes, stream of consciousness rants and ideas on how to take my life in a better direction. A family member began sending me Buddhist literature and I started to meditate. This was the beginning of a major life change for me. The steps taken in those days have directly led to my present space.

While I wrote mountains of manifestations, I began to notice my handwriting becoming slower, more precise. As my thoughts slowed down and reflection became the norm, my physical world started to reflect the internal changes. Learning to meditate in an environment filled with false-ego and posturing was not an easy task. I persisted and found many moments of peace despite being physically caged.

In the years following my incarceration I struggled to stay connected to that feeling of pure being, of truly being in the moment and accepting that I could not control the outside world. The best I could do was to work on my spirit. When I would slip, I'd pick myself back up. Eventually I found myself released from parole and creating a new life, with a new passion for knowledge and community.

In 2011 I decided to complete my journey and celebrate my new sense of freedom by taking a cross-country bicycle tour. I had long been plotting an adventure that would give me the ultimate sense of a restriction-less lifestyle and the wonder that comes with the open road. I took my bike, some books and some supplies and traveled across Texas and into New Mexico. For three months I camped, rode and volunteered on farms.

It was during this time that I once again found myself humbled by the lessons that came my way. I met many beautiful people who each imparted a bit of their own experience to me. I slept under more stars than I had ever seen, howling along with the coyotes and laughing at how dirty but free I was. In those three months I laughed, I cried, I challenged myself like never before, and decided to see every part of the journey as a magnificent piece of the puzzle waiting for me to put it together.

I remembered the peace that I had found while behind razor wire and recognized how the isolation had allowed my mind to receive clarity and be washed clean. It was these two experiences that have played the most significant role in my awakening and growth. When given the time with my own mind, whether by force or choice, I began to understand my fears and my hopes. I saw my failures and witnessed the destructive nature of my past actions. I had a vision of a crossroads, a divided road. One way would take me further into darkness and the other could be the journey of a lifetime. I have pondered long and hard, asking myself what it is about these two unique experiences that sparked a quest within.

I have found that I, like many modern humans, was living a busy life filled with plenty of ways to ignore myself and slap on a façade of joy and happiness. I found that I had been doing anything and everything possible to avoid sitting down for five minutes and communicating with my own mind. I had lost touch with whom I identified as my self. And in the process had lost a connection with my own humanity and heart. By having no other option but to sit, in a prison bed or on an isolated back road, I had an opportunity to understand my deepest pains and to begin healing them. It is this healing that will help bring our species back in alignment with the planet and its inhabitants.

Learning to Find Balance

Humans seek refuge from the big city in a number of ways. We take weekend camping trips to get away from the light and noise pollution, the smog and the people. As much as we are communal creatures with a desire to form relationships, we also seek to break away and reconnect with nature and the simple life. In those spaces we find the time to sit with ourselves and begin "checking in" with our mind to form healthy relationships with those closest to us.

The history books are filled with stories of individuals who sought out the rugged, dangerous, lonely, beautiful life that the solitary road offers. From Everett Reuss to Christopher McCandless, humans have pursued adventure and communion with nature for a variety of reasons. Many of these adventurers (myself included) have learned that community and familial experiences are equally as important as our personal vision quests. Life is balance. If you find yourself in the company of others solely to avoid dealing with your personal situations and hard truths, it might be time to spend a weekend alone. On the other hand, if you have spent the majority of your time in quiet reflection, try going out into the community and making connections with other people.

In the end we are each other's greatest asset for finding out what freedom means, how to achieve it and what role the global community will play. By opting to spend time examining ourselves, we become more capable of having positive, encouraging relationships and helping those who may be struggling to know themselves. For me, it was these two experiences that allowed me to discover the empowerment that waited in quiet contemplation. Being behind bars and in the wilderness also showed me that regardless of where I was in the physical sense, happiness, and thus liberation, could be attained by choosing to go within.

Indigenous people from a variety of cultures have understood and taught the power of solitude and the necessity of journeying. "Vision Quests" may take place in a myriad of forms – in the physical world involving several days or weeks of surviving amongst the elements; or something internal such as a deeply introspective meditation session fostered by repetitive drums, rattles, and chants. Whether a physical or mental journey, they represent a quest for knowledge and understanding of the self and how it relates to the physical and spiritual worlds.

As we move from activity to activity in our busy daily lives, we often ignore or forget pains and valuable insights we have gathered along our path. By taking time to do the difficult work of self-examination and healing, we contribute to making our individual lives more enjoyable, and encourage others to go within. By promoting a more balanced state of mind and spirit, we are contributing to the cause of freedom and helping create a more compassionate tomorrow.

Chapter 9 - Are We All One? Collectivism vs. Individuality

"We are all one" is a phrase often spoken in spiritual circles to describe the interconnectedness of all life on the planet - human, plant, animal, insect and beyond. Many anarchists who value their individuality and free choice tend to be apprehensive about this seemingly collectivist worldview. However, it is possible for one to believe in a path that is in harmony with nature and its creatures, while simultaneously believing in the right to be a free individual and freedom of association.

Throughout most of the world, people are taught to look at reality in a very polarized way. When certain issues are presented to us through mainstream circles, they are usually oversimplified to the point of being a black or white concept– all people are either good or bad, with no in between. In reality, life is much more complicated than that. There are usually many different ways of looking at a situation and many different sides to any story.

This is especially true in the study of philosophy because terms are constantly being redefined and ideas constantly reexamined with every new generation of philosophers to accommodate the new insight and information that has become available over time.

One concept that is vastly misunderstood and oversimplified by the general population is that of individualism and collectivism. While there are many different ideas about what these words mean, the true value of any concept is determined by the consequences that arise in society as a result of its implementation.

At face value, collectivism has been a philosophy with cheery rhetoric, but horrible outcomes. This is because it has traditionally been implemented coercively through politics. Collectivist philosophers have spoken of noble goals like making sacrifices for the group and working together and cooperating. They have said these are things that people should do. It very well may be true that people should behave in these ways, but the problem is that politicians come along and use this philosophy as a way of telling people what they must do.

The mainstream stereotype of an individualist is someone who is a selfish person with no desire to participate in the community at all. The contrasting view of a collectivist is someone who cares about the tribe as a whole, so much so that they are willing to sacrifice their own well-being for the sake of the tribe. Individualism has nothing to do with selfishness. It is simply a way of looking at people without separating them into various groups by race, nationality, gender, religion or social status.

When people are seen as groups instead of individuals, large numbers of people are often held responsible for things that individuals among them have done. There is also a great danger in the idea that an individual needs permission from the group to exercise his or her own free will, which is exactly the type of worldview on which collectivist concepts like "democracy" and "consensus" were built.

We have often found that well-meaning spiritually inclined individuals buy into "New Age" messages that operate under the guise of helping out the whole human species. This could be a small group of wealthy individuals promoting a reduction in the population, or forced sterilization for the supposed good of the whole. An Anarchist perusing some modern spiritual material might be turned off by the prevalence of statist and collectivist language. Compassionate individuals may find themselves wrapped up in philosophies that claim to be about a greater good but end up harming the individual and thus the community as a whole. Anarchists may be so independent they completely ignore the importance of community and turn away those who want liberation for all.

It's time we recognize each individual as a sacred being. To respect the whole, we must first respect the individual. For an individual to be truly free, he or she must not have physical obligations to anyone else. Rather an individual must be able to freely choose who to interact with in a meaningful and peaceful way. In this manner he or she can then become truly fulfilled and free. At the very least, mutual respect for other free individuals' life choices will go a long way.

One of the most powerful examples of interdependence comes from the Avataṃsaka Sūtra of the Mahayana Buddhist philosophy. The Huayan, or Flower Garland School of Mahayana, was founded on the ideas expressed in the Avataṃsaka Sūtra, also known as the Flower Garland Sutra or

Flower Ornament Scripture. This sutra centers on the ideas of interdependence and an interpenetrating reality. It describes worlds upon worlds, overlapping and coexisting within each other.

This concept is best expressed in the story of the jeweled net of Indra. Indra was a God who was said to possess a net that extended infinitely in all directions. The net contained individual shimmering diamonds that spread out in all directions. Each individual diamond was perfect on its own, but the individual pieces also reflected the beauty and light of the surrounding diamonds.

Thomas Cleary, a renowned translator of Eastern texts, describes the beauty of the tale of Indra's net in his book Entry Into the Inconceivable: An Introduction to Hua-Yen Buddhism. Cleary writes:

"The seventh gate is called the realm of Indra's net. The net of Indra is a net of jewels: not only does each jewel reflect all the other jewels but the reflections of all the jewels in each jewel also contain the reflections of all the other jewels, ad infinitum. This "infinity of infinities" represents the interidentification and interpenetration of all things as illustrated in the preceding gates.

To illustrate the net of Indra principle with a simplistic example from everyday life, we might consider the cost of a commodity as representing a nexus of various conditions. For the sake of simplicity, let us say the cost of something reflects (1) the cost of raw materials, (2) the cost of energy required for its manufacture, (3) the cost of labor involved in its production, and (4) the cost of transportation for distribution.

Turning our attention to raw materials, the first element, we can see that the cost of raw materials also involves the cost of energy required for their extraction, the cost of labor involved in their extraction, and the cost of transportation of the raw materials to the processing site. The cost of energy involves the cost of raw materials from which energy is produced as well as raw materials for the devices involved, the cost of labor involved in producing energy, and the cost of distribution of energy. The cost of labor reflects the cost of goods, energy, and transportation necessary for the work force. The cost of transportation involves the cost of materials, energy, and labor necessary to the manufacture and operation of transportation systems. Thus each element in this analysis reflects and contains every other element.

While this example is rudimentary, using an oversimplified scheme of analysis and stopping at only one level of subanalysis, it illustrates how the net of Indra concept may be applied to the development of a balanced view of a complex of phenomena. The analytic framework may be usefully applied in economics, socioeconomics, group and individual psychology, and ecology. While it may be said that the net of Indra does not necessarily reveal anything startlingly new- it is, after all, merely an articulation of a principle inherent in an interdependent nexus of phenomena- still it is a valuable instrument for the achievement of balance and depth in understanding and, moreover, for the avoidance of one-sided views, " (pages 37, 38).

We see value in understanding this parable and its call for unity without ignoring diversity. The sutra paints an image of a world in which one is simultaneously dependent on others and depended on by others. The whole is considered in relation to each individual and each individual is seen in relation to other individuals. Again, Cleary offers clarity...

"The ethic of the Hua-yen teaching is based on this fundamental theme of universal interdependence; while the so-called bodhisattva, the person devoted to enlightenment, constantly nourishes aspiration and will going beyond the world, nevertheless the striving for completion and perfection, the development of ever greater awareness, knowledge, freedom, and capability, is continually reinvested, as it were, in the world, dedicated to the liberation and enlightenment of all beings." (page 2).

While Huayan Buddhism hints at the power of interdependence and the importance of the individual, certain native communities believe that individuality in the western world has played a role in the breaking down of the social fabric. While we cannot deny that a lack of awareness and concern for the fellow humans in the global community allows certain individuals to make destructive choices, we believe overall that the individual and the community are both valuable. You should not necessarily give yourself up to the will of the collective, but remain willing to examine your individual behavior and recognize whether you are doing more harm than good.

Since we share this planet with billions of humans, animals, plants, stones, and countless other life forms it is advisable to find ways to work together. We are connected through DNA, through our energetic bodies and through our current position in time and space. By learning to value and love ourselves we can move to a place of valuing and loving those with whom we share our local and global communities.

Chapter 10 - Balancing the Feminine and the Masculine

As we have noted, many of the world's problems are physical manifestations of a lack of internal healing. State institutions have no trouble manipulating large portions of the population that are too lost in their own emotional muck to pay attention to the oppression happening all around them. This can be seen clearly in the division that has taken place over generations between the genders. Only by working through our individual emotional traumas can we heal and begin to create a more free world.

For millennia the human species has been pitted against each other. When brute strength was the only requirement to rule over another life, men would kill and enslave each other and often take women as slaves, using force to meet their every need. This imbalanced state, combined with the disconnect from Nature we have discussed, created a world full of inequality and pain. Historically, governments and the prevailing attitudes of the populace promoted the idea that women were inferior. This is evident in fathers owning their wives and daughters, and the fact that women were not allowed to own property or make any choices of their own.

Anthropological evidence indicates that societies operated in a much more Egalitarian fashion before the innovation of agriculture and domestication of communities. In "*The Origins of Fatherhood: An Ancient Family Process*" Sebastian Kraemer writes that the Patriarchal mindset came about around 6,000 years ago with the growing concept of fatherhood. Even the great philosopher Aristotle believed women were inferior to men in intellect, morality and physical ability. Regardless of how it began, we can clearly see an imbalance in the way women have been treated for thousands of years. To be fair, most people on this planet, of either gender, have been subject to enslavement by whatever authority ruled over their particular landmass, but even amongst other male slaves throughout history, the pervading attitude was that women deserved no rights.

However, there have been exceptions to this point of view. Greek historian Herodotus wrote about the differences between Egyptian and Greek women, specifically Egyptian women who maintained employment in a variety of trades. He noted that Egyptian women were often found in

positions of power, able to inherit property and able to secure loans–
privileges unheard of for women in Greece in Herodotus' time.

There is a rich history of Goddess and femininity worship. There are
thousands of female statues dating back 5,000 years before the Current
Era, found in the Mehrgarh area of Pakistan, as well as a Mother Goddess
statue in India that has been carbon-dated to 20,000 years before the
Current Era. These seem to indicate a certain respect, if not worship, of
the feminine form. Examples of female deities can be found all over the
world.

The Pueblo and Hopi peoples of the American Southwest speak of a Great
Mother who helped create the stars and the sky. In Inca mythology there is
Pachamama, a fertility goddess who watches over the Earth and harvests.

There is also Shaktism, a branch of Hinduism that focuses devotional
efforts on Shakti or Devi, the Hindu Divine Mother. In ancient Greece,
Gaia was the name of the mother of all life, the great Greek Mother
Goddess who gave birth to the Earth and the universe. More recently we
have Goddess movements such as Dianicc Wicca and terms like "Sacred"
or "Divine" Feminine, a New Age spin on the Hindu Shakti teachings.

Despite isolated historical examples of equality, the dominant mentality
has been one of male supremacy. Rejection of this system and pursuit of
equality is known as Feminism. At various points in history, women and
men have both sought to empower women and establish practices of
equality. Although there have been discussions of equal rights since the
14th century, there is no agreed upon beginning of the Feminist
philosophy. Most scholars agree that American Feminism has had three
waves, each concerned with different aspects of freedom for Women. The
first wave of Feminism came in the 18th and 19th centuries and focused
on "Women's Suffrage", the right of women to vote and hold political
office. In America, the Women's Suffrage movement began gaining
ground in the 18th Century as women pursued the right to vote. Second-
Wave feminism came about during the 1960's until the 1980's, and
broadened its focus to examine gender roles and culturally ingrained
inequalities. The Third-Wave, and current phase of Feminism includes a
wide range of philosophies, including rejections of past schools of

feminist thought, as well as evolutions of First and Second-Wave feminism.

Out of the struggles of Second-Wave of feminism emerged Radical Feminism. Radical Feminism focused on dismantling Patriarchy through opposition of gender roles. It considered how social class, race, sexual preference and socioeconomic status play into the treatment of women and men. Many Radical Feminists had prior experience in the Civil Rights battles of the 1960's. These movements were focused on direct action and did not necessarily push for political solutions to the inequalities they opposed.

In the late 19th and early 20th centuries, American Feminism merged with the principles of Anarchy to form what some call Anarcha-Feminism. Prominent Anarchist thinker Emma Goldman is seen as a founder of Anarcha-Feminism. For Goldman, the opposition to male supremacy was essential in the struggle against State power. She was also a huge advocate of reproductive rights, sex education, and access to contraception. Before many other radicals accepted homosexuality, Goldman was publicly defending the rights of gay men and lesbian women to love as they pleased.

Goldman criticized voting as a legitimate form of fighting the State. She believed it foolish to assume that giving women the right to vote would halt the crimes of the State. "*To assume, therefore, that she would succeed in purifying something which is not susceptible of purification, is to credit her with supernatural powers,*" she wrote in "*Womans Suffrage*".

Another prominent figure in American Anarcha-Feminism was Voltairine de Cleyre. De Cleyre was critical of traditional beauty ideals, gender roles, and the marriage laws that allowed men to rape their wives without fear of legal consequence. She wrote for Benjamin Tucker's classic newsletter Liberty. In addition to being a feminist, Voltairine was an advocate of Anarchism without adjectives. In her 1901 essay, Anarchism, she writes of the need for Anarchists of all economic schools to work together in free experimentation. She concludes, "*There is nothing un-Anarchistic about any of them until the element of compulsion enters and obliges unwilling persons to remain in a community whose economic arrangements they do not agree to."*

One of the more contentious areas that Feminists have explored is the question of whether gender roles are a valid concept or simply a social construct. Western cultures tend to accept two genders, male or female, while cultures around the world, throughout history, have accepted three or more genders. These include the mahu of the Kanaka Maoli indigenous. The mahu were seen as sacred educators of ancient traditions and could be either male or female with a gender somewhere in between or sharing traits both masculine and feminine. Among the Bugi people of the Sulawesi island of Indonesia, five genders are recognized. The Bugi support the idea of men, women, calabai, calalai, and bissu. Calabai are biological males who take on the role of a heterosexual female. Their dress and gender expression are feminine. Calalai are biological females who identify with a male gender. Bissu are healers or mediums who "transcend" gender and encompass aspects of all five in order to form a whole. Several American Indian tribes also have similar concepts. The Lakota word Winyanktehca can be translated as "two-souls-person", or "to be as a woman". The term is applied to biological males who are transgender. The "winkte" are an important part of the spiritual community. The Navajo also have a similar concept in the Nádleehí, which could be translated as "one who constantly transforms".

Roles are imposed on each gender according to certain qualities that are deemed acceptable and those that are not. Queer theory proposes a deconstruction of gender-identity to get to the roots of oppression.

Psychologist Cordelia Fine believes there are inherent biological differences between the minds of men and women. However, she also believes that cultural traditions are responsible for shaping these apparent differences between the sexes. Professor Dianne Halpern writes that social and biological factors are equally responsible and cannot be separated. In Sex Differences in Cognitive Abilities, Halpern writes that cultural traditions and biology both play a role in determining gender identity. She discusses how the influence of testosterone on a male brain gives men a slight advantage in tasks such as building with blocks. This could lead a male to seek opportunities to exercise similar skills, such as sports. Over time these activities are labeled as male specific and become ingrained into the culture itself. However, these culturally accepted norms are not absolute and should not be used as a barometer for socially accepted behavior by either sex.

We believe a conversation on balancing the feminine and masculine is incomplete without discussing gender roles as possible tools for oppression of the freedom of expression and the freedom to love. The idea that all men are supposed to be tough, brave, fearless and unemotional has caused untold harm to the human race. Just as dangerous is the idea that all women are to be emotionally open, compassionate, easily scared, delicate, and passive. These concepts reinforce division among the masses and allow the authorities to pit men and women against each other. Rather than seeing each other as equals capable of great things, we are taught to buy into and support false versions of the Male-Female dynamic. We also support transgendered individuals who may have been born with sex organs that do not correspond to the gender role they associate with. Culturally reinforced ideas on the types of relationships that are acceptable have also caused harm to human relationships.

Not only have our roles in society been predetermined by those in positions of authority, but our private relationships with one another have also been heavily controlled. For centuries church and state have dictated what human relationships should look like based on their own political interests. In the past this control was more apparent with arranged marriages and laws against certain types of partnerships. Even today remnants of these traditions still exist. For example, marriage licenses still prevent people of the same gender from being legally recognized as a couple in 13 states (with 37 states allowing legal same sex marriage), just as those same licenses prevented interracial marriage until 1967. The societal norms regarding relationships are still heavily rooted in traditions that were created by figures of authority many ages ago.

One of the most obvious examples of an ancient tradition controlling modern relationships is that of monogamy, the idea that a male-female partnership requires each person to abstain from all other sexual activity. This is something that many people prefer, which is great for them, but this is a path that should be freely chosen by each participant in the relationship, instead of an assumed prerequisite. When entering relationships, the vast majority of people simply go through the motions and do what society expects of them, without ever stopping to discuss or even consider that they have the freedom to decide what their relationship will look like, as long as each person is on the same page. When given the option, some people would choose monogamy, while others may choose polyamory, a philosophy that allows for multiple sexual partners. It does not matter which path is chosen– what matters is that each person in the relationship was able to freely choose the framework of their partnership.

For all of its merits and successes in the last hundred years, some would argue that Feminism in the Internet age has become divisive. Modern American Feminists have been criticized for promoting "Female Supremacy" rather than equality. While some feminists may lobby for government granted privileges in the name of Feminism, Anarcha-Feminists truly seek equality. Other criticisms include accusations of First World feminists forgetting about their struggling counterparts in Third World nations who are also dealing with oppressive, Patriarchal regimes.

There is also the tendency for feminists to use the State to enforce equality. An Anarchist view of Feminism recognizes that the State does more harm than good by reinforcing traditional gender roles. The State pushes the idea that a liberated woman is a woman who has joined the workforce, pays taxes, and votes for her master. Governments love to declare that liberation has been achieved by incorporating women into their tax farm. We work towards acceptance of all individual choices, not declarations of equality enforced by governments. One reason women may be inclined to trust and seek assistance from government support systems is a seeming lack of private alternatives. This is why building and creating alternative institutions that recognize the value of all life, regardless of sexual orientation, gender or race, is of the utmost importance. Efforts to use the government as a tool for equality have often resulted in "state feminism", which uses the force of government to grant rights and outlaw discrimination based on gender. This often leads to other forms of control, including limiting the free speech of important feminist leaders who are critical of government policies.

Men and women have been divided throughout our history on this planet. We have also experienced periods of great unity. The human species will benefit immensely from promotion of free expression of love and acceptance of all individual's right to live their lives to their contentment.

To achieve this goal we must eradicate institutionalized oppression, including Patriarchy. Still, the answer to millennia of abuse towards women is not shaming and condemning men. Once again, we stress the importance of balance. We support individual accountability, education and expulsion of bigots of all types. If we are to truly move past these divisive and harmful ideas, we must begin to accept the role we each play in allowing the oppression of the opposite sex. Only as well-adjusted, emotionally-balanced individuals can we create a truly free and compassionate society that respects all life.

Part 2: Anti-Authoritarianism in World Traditions

In the following chapters we will explore some of the popular spiritual traditions of the world to find their anti-authoritarian roots. We will also consider how these traditions were, in many cases, institutionalized and turned into systems of control in the form of religion.

The ideas that we cover in this book are merely scratching the surface and are intended to jumpstart a conversation that is long overdue. We admit that in some areas we possess limited knowledge, so we are approaching these topics as students with curiosity and are more than happy to have other people expand on these ideas.

There are some cultures that we simply do not know enough about to speak on with confidence. With some cultures, such as the Vedic and Judaic traditions, we were not able to find adequate selections, so there remains plenty of room for improvement in this study.

Chapter 11 - Intersections of Shamanism and Anarchism

A discussion on the concepts of freedom would not be complete without an understanding of the Shaman and his spiritual teachings. A Shaman is quite simply a teacher and a student. A shaman is an individual who uses a variety of methods to communicate with the universe and the spiritual world. Shamans have been known as leaders of the community and communicators of divine messages for personal growth. A Shaman experiences "religious ecstasy" when he or she accesses realms unseen to the physical world.

Shamans are said to travel between the physical and spiritual world to bring back knowledge for themselves and the community. Some actions taken by a Shaman include tunneling to an underworld of spirits, experiencing altered states through drumming, meditation or ingesting substances such as plant concoctions, and healing ailments by finding the root cause on the spiritual plane.

We want to be clear that these definitions are based on our experience with Shamanic practices. The truth is, anthropologists themselves do not have one accepted definition for the term. Some define Shamans as anyone who accesses the spirit world in altered states of consciousness, while others compare Shamans to witch doctors or prophets. Others define Shamans as schizophrenics.

The term itself has been attributed to the Evenki word saman spoken by the indigenous peoples of Siberia. The word is thought by some scholars to mean, "to know", however this and the true origin of the word are often contested.

Some critics of the word believe it to be a racist umbrella term that ignores the vast amount of belief systems that exist underneath it. In the same way the term Native American has been applied to all indigenous peoples of the North American landmass, the term Shamanism is insufficient when describing such vastly different peoples and ideas. Most indigenous cultures do not even have a word for Shaman. We use the term with respect to all the beautifully diverse cultures that are categorized as Shamanism.

Western Europe and the Americas were first introduced to the term in the late 17th century. No one really knows when Shamanism began. We find that the lack of a solid definition and origin reaffirms our belief that Shamanism predates all modern religions.

Shamanism has been called the aboriginal root of religion. All over the world throughout history, aborigines were deeply connected to nature and used practices some of us in the modern world would consider insane. Through the use of hallucinogenic plants, drums or meditation, one could experience a spiritual cleansing and a connection to a deeper understanding of self. This is also done through shamanic journeys–deeply personal journeys sometimes performed in the mind and sometimes performed in the wilderness for days or weeks.

Looking at anthropological studies of shamanism from cultures around the world, one finds an amazing connection to Anarchy. In "Shamans Path", controversial anthropologist Michael Harner details why Shamanism was a threat to the ruling classes:

"A reason it was wiped out is because it undermines the authority of the state and church. To have hundreds of thousands of prophets running around on the loose, in shamanism everyone is his or her own prophet, getting spiritual validation directly from the highest sources. Such people rock the boat; they are subversive. After all, if everyone is an authority, there is little possibility of creating a monopolistic business based on privileged access or right to interpret the words of a few official prophets or holy books." ("What is a Shaman?" in Shamans Path, page 10).

Shamanism is Anarchy of the spiritual world. In the same way that the State authorities fear an educated, organized populace, the Church authorities fear an independent, spiritually aware congregation. With its loose traditions and models for connecting to the realm beyond the five senses, Shamanism completely bypasses the monopoly on God encouraged by all political church bodies. Since Shamanism predates the modern church, it is actually the religious establishment that has been the aggressor against the free spirited pursuits of Shamans.

A wide variety of ancient cultures held beliefs that fell within the realm of Shamanism. From the indigenous tribes of America to the Celtic tribes of Western Europe, ancient civilizations shared many commonalities in their spiritual practices.

Before royal oligarchies gave spirituality a strict set of rules and guidelines, indigenous cultures had a much more personal and open religious tradition. Through Shamanism these cultures were able to advance their spiritual knowledge with every age that passed, because each generation played an active role in building their culture's understanding of the universe. Much how our scientific research is conducted today, generation after generation would put in work to slowly chip away at the mysteries they were trying to uncover.

Shamanism operates in a similar way, but it deals with exploring the realm of the spirit, instead of the material realm of science. Generations of scientific research have allowed our species to create incredible technology, but our spiritual growth is absolutely crippled due to lack of exploration.

For the last few thousand years, much of the modern world has stopped exploring the spirit realm. The religious institutions that have had control of the spiritual dialogue for the past few millennia have completely forbidden any kind of research into these realms.

They tell us there are no new questions to be asked because they already have all the answers and to ask any kind of question is heresy. It is this kind of strict stubbornness and arrogance that has caused much of our generation's complete disinterest in spirituality. The fact that these institutions are trying to keep us from asking questions should tell us that they are not to be trusted. They do not want us thinking philosophically because it could threaten their political power and influence.

Shamanism is different from our modern religious institutions because there is no agenda or hierarchy. There are no cloaked figures to tell you that you are not worthy and then take your money. There is no inquisition to condemn you to death if you happen to disagree with someone else's metaphysical conclusion. There are no politics or heretics. No one is going to benefit from you financially or tell you how to think. No one is going to call you evil or demand that you be killed because you don't comply with his or her edict.

Shamanism is less of a belief system and more of an advanced form of philosophy. Belief systems often claim to have every single correct answer in the universe, which can have a negative impact on society. If people believe there are no intellectual frontiers, they will stop looking and stop questioning. When this happens, they are cutting themselves short. Major human advancements result from individuals trying to expand the collective pool of knowledge– not from recycling the information handed down by authoritarians for centuries.

Life is a mystery, forever unraveling. Every time a question about our universe is answered, ten more surface in its place. Even if one were to live for a hundred years in daily research and meditation, he or she would still have questions. There would still be more left to uncover.

Every great teacher that has walked this earth has recognized the infinite mystery of life. This is the kind of attitude that is necessary to investigate the spirit world through shamanism. This path will not give you a prepackaged set of ideals and convictions wrapped with a bow and carried by a savior. You will be forced to create your own belief structure that will change every day with every new situation you encounter. It shouldn't even have a name. The fact that we even call it "Shamanism" is simply because we have to attach a term to the philosophy in order to articulate the idea. Spirituality is a personal experience that should be a respected mutual interest between all humanity, instead of a barrier.

It is important to point out that not all Shaman traditions have been free and peaceful. As with all spiritual traditions, there have been individuals who have claimed to have a direct connection with the divine and have exacted authority over others. This has resulted in many brutal Shaman regimes where human sacrifice, war, and slavery were all common practices. These practices, which violate natural law through aggression, are considered "Dark Shamanism". This is a common theme that you will notice throughout this whole book: spiritual belief can be used for great healing when an individual has a connection with the universe, or with god, or with their deepest self. However, spiritual belief can also create unimaginable harm when individuals and organizations act as gatekeepers for that connection.

We want to take a moment to note two important terms when dealing with Shamanism in the modern age. These are "Plastic Shamans" and "NeoShamans".

A plastic shaman is as another term for a snake oil salesman, or someone who sells fraudulent products or promotes their work as something it is not. In this case it applies to those who purport to be of indigenous descent or have learned native ways, yet have no direct involvement.

Furthermore, a plastic shaman is someone who sells native knowledge or alleged teachings in exchange for profit. Selling sacred teachings is extremely frowned upon and disrespectful. Many Native communities in America see the modern world's appropriation of indigenous teachings as another form of colonialism. A plastic shaman will claim that he or she can teach you a lifetime of understanding in a weekend - if you just pay the right price. A plastic shaman may have learned a thing or two from a Native community to sell the lessons to curious, unaware suburban folk. Not only is this a detriment to the communities, but also to the seekers themselves who learn false teachings and likely spread those false ideas to other inquisitive minds.

This appropriation of culture has caused several tribes and assemblies to declare war against plastic shamans. On June 10, 1993, Lakota, Dakota and Nakota nations from the United States and Canada met at the Lakota Summit V. At this gathering, around 500 representatives, from 40 different tribes and bands of Lakota, unanimously passed the "*Declaration of War Against Exploiters of Lakota Spirituality*." The declaration contains the following statement:

"We assert a posture of zero-tolerance for any "white man's shaman" who rises from within our own communities to "authorize" the expropriation of our ceremonial ways by non-Indians; all such "*plastic medicine men*" *are enemies of the Lakota, Dakota and Nakota people.*"

This statement from the *"Resolution of the 5th Annual Meeting of the Traditional Elders Circle"* drafted by several nations at Camp Rosebud Creek, Montana on October 5, 1980, amends this strong stance.

"We concern ourselves only with those people who use spiritual ceremonies with non-Indian people for profit. There are many things to be shared with the Four Colors of humanity in our common destiny as one with our Mother the Earth. It is this sharing that must be considered with great care by the Elders and the medicine people who carry the Sacred Trusts, so that no harm may come to people through ignorance and misuse of these powerful forces."

In this spirit of cooperation, we hope to learn from diverse Native cultures and evolve with respect to their ancient teachings, while incorporating newly discovered forms of healing. This brings us to the topic of NeoShamans. NeoShamanism describes modern interpretations of older forms of shamanism and traditional teachings. NeoShamanism is not a single set of beliefs, but a variety of ways to attain altered states of mind and commune with the spirit world.

A NeoShaman may be a non-native and have no connection to any past tribe. Rather, the NeoShaman absorbs knowledge from many places and incorporates the individual pieces into a tapestry of spiritual awareness.

With the advent of computers and rapidly expanding technologies, many students of Shamanism have learned to alter their states of consciousness, for the purpose of healing, using computers, binaural beats and other non-traditional methods. The terms "Techno-Shaman" and "Crypto-Shaman" have even come into use in recent years.

What is the difference between a Plastic Shaman and a NeoShaman? This is a matter of great debate and personal opinion. We believe that encouraging peoples from around the world to share and learn from one another is a positive action that will propel humanity forward, not backward. However, we understand that many Native communities look back at the history of relations between themselves and outsiders and have little desire to invite the Western world into their sacred teachings. We respect these decisions and hope that Non-Natives interested in learning sative ways seek out Native teachers with tribe affiliation and a true understanding of the culture. We also hope those interested in spirituality and shamanism are able to learn from many sources and decide which path to God/Source/Self-Actualization resonates the strongest.

As long as we learn with an open mind and do not to speak for tribes, peoples, and cultures in which we are not well versed, we can build bridges between these diverse worlds without destroying the individual cultures. In fact, the idea of keeping a powerful interpretation of god and the Universe all to a small group of people rings of elitism. At the same time it is up to each community and each individual to decide what teachings they share and with whom.

The fact that various groups of aristocrats from different cultural backgrounds have managed to stamp a copyright on spirituality is itself a complete sacrilege. Everyone should have their own religion that they ponder on and share. If more people proclaimed their beliefs aloud, the good ideas would be more likely to surface and become more popular, while the bad ideas would dwindle off rather easily. The best ideas would be passed along to the next generation and molded based on whatever new information came in during that time. This shamanic worldview would be a constantly changing collective religion actually built by everyone in society. This would eliminate a lot of the spiritual segregation that is caused by modern religion, because participants would be encouraged to learn from one another instead of look down on one another.

If people spoke to each other philosophically on a regular basis and reached into the spirit realm using meditation and psychedelics, we would be able to achieve the same kind of breakthroughs in the spirit realm that we have in the material realm, bringing us much closer to peace.

Chapter 12 - Intersections of Christianity and Anarchism

There is no doubt that unimaginable suffering and division have been caused by the political organizations that formed around Christianity, Judaism, Islam and the other religions of the world. However, as we intend to explore in the following chapters, there is ample evidence suggesting that these religions all carry knowledge from similar ancient teachings, but sadly the hierarchies of these organized religions have perverted these teachings according to the politics of the time.

The biblical accounts of Jesus were not consolidated and printed until roughly 300 years after his death. At that time, his followers had caused a massive social upheaval which threatened the established religious institutions. Even in his own time, Jesus was an enemy of the state and an enemy of the church for his radical views of peace, freedom and equality. The established religious order of the time was the Roman church and they were so threatened by his philosophy that they had him silenced. However, his death did not silence his message and his ideas spread all over the empire. Fearful that this anti-establishment movement would break down their spiritual monopoly, the church developed a plan to corrupt the message of Christ and use his cult status as a banner for their religious institution.

The religious institution responsible for the death of Christ and the persecution of his followers was now planning to merge his popular image with their dogmatic tradition. In 325 AD the Roman Church held *"The Council of Nicaea"*, a meeting of ranking church figures. Here they discussed how they would deal with the explosion of the Christian philosophy in their society. The church knew that if they let things continue as they were, all of their subjects would convert to Christianity in a very short time. They had to find a way to subvert this trend and convert the Christians back to the traditional structure to maintain control. To achieve this goal, the establishment decided to merge Christian teachings with their own in such a way that the radical message of peace and freedom was replaced with the hierarchy of the existing church. The outcome of the Council of Nicaea stated that Jesus Christ was the son of god and that he was to be treated as a divine figure. This went again Christ's insistence that he was only a messenger and that people should follow his message, not worship him. There is a great deal of controversy surrounding the divinity of Christ and many say that he didn't want organized churches in his name.

Christian followers, who mostly belonged to the working illiterate class, were deceived by the church and felt that this was a cause to celebrate, because the church had finally formally recognized their savior. Most Christians did not understand the true implications of the terms that their rulers laid out at the Council of Nicaea. The church then used "the divinity of Christ" as supporting evidence for all of their philosophies, even though the issue of divinity had been decided at the conference.

With the image and following of Jesus now a part of their church, the establishment was able to neutralize the social movement of Christianity from within. Once the church molded the Christian ideologies to fit its own political agenda, it was also able to dictate an "official" but corrupted recording of history. The church focused only on their fabricated depictions of Christ's birth and death and gave very little mention of what he actually stood for and what he did throughout his life. Many historical accounts of Jesus have been suppressed by the religious institutions, because the reality of his political struggle would expose many of the primary falsehoods of our authoritarian society.

This is the way the establishment has "watered down" and misdirected the revolutionary message of Jesus. This is the most successful strategy of silencing and corrupting revolutionary movements, which is used by the ruling class when they are backed up against a wall. They know that attempts to fully eradicate a social movement would only make that movement stronger and give it more credibility, so they simply corrupt the message and turn it into a tool of social control. Even in the accounts of Jesus that have not been destroyed by the church, we can see his extremely obvious opposition towards the oppressive systems of government, banking and organized religion. In all of the biblical depictions of Christ he has a peaceful state of mind, except when he is dealing with "the money changers".

According to biblical writings, Jesus used physical force to throw the money changers out of a temple, which was the only account of his ever getting physical with anyone. The money changers were an ancient banking cartel that ruled the ancient world by lending money to governments and applying interest. Just like today, the money changers of biblical times were deeply embedded in the government.

Behind the fabricated image of Jesus that the church has been perpetuating for centuries, there is most likely a revolutionary who vehemently opposed the ruling class and fought for the rights of the oppressed throughout his life. His whole life was a struggle for peace, equality and human rights, yet the religions that have sprung up in his name have distorted his message, because it stands against blind obedience to authority. Whether or not Jesus Christ was a divine being, a human revolutionary or a character of astrotheology is not for the authors of this book to decide. That is a matter for people to decide based upon their own studies. Regardless, the message of compassion, non-aggression and anti-authoritarianism behind the story of Jesus Christ remains the same.

Since Jesus's time, political organizations in the form of religions have carried on his image, but they have largely abandoned his message. That being said, there have been a number of Christian thinkers with very strong anti-authoritarian views and a number of Christian movements with very strong anarchist traits. Within just a few generations of the Council of Nicea, Saint Augustine was quick to point out that the teachings of Christ were in total opposition to the values of the Roman Empire and the Roman church. In present times there are Christian churches spread throughout the United States that have recognized the same thing. Sadly, there are still many war-mongering neo-conservative churches as well.

The Quakers are an entire sect of Christianity that is openly anti-authoritarian. The Quakers are also the group with the deepest history of both activism and anarchist philosophy. Sadly, in mainstream thought, Quakers are often confused with the Puritans, a sect of Christianity in colonial America that was known for being repressive and tyrannical. The Quakers and the Puritans had two totally different schools of thought– the Puritans believed the bible granted religious organizations authority over human beings, while the Quakers believed each individual was capable of forming his or her own connection with god and that there was no need for an external authority. The only reason these groups are often confused is because they are both Christian sects that escaped England for the new world, but in all other respects they could not be more different from one another. The Quakers do not recognize human authority. In fact, authority isn't even a part of their vocabulary. For example, Quakers will not refer to a person by a title, such as judge, officer, president, your highness, your honor, your majesty or any of the terms that groveling peasants are coerced into repeating. The Quakers also played an essential role in the abolition movement and the Underground Railroad, and many of the civil rights struggles that followed.

By studying the history of the figure that is Jesus Christ and the traditions that arose following his death, it is clear that his message has become distorted and corrupted. Perhaps all that is needed is for followers of Christ to abandon the churches and leaders who claim to have the path to his teachings and instead cultivate their own personal conversation with him and individually interpret his message.

Chapter 13 - Intersections of Islam and Anarchism

The following are two guest essays selected from Davi Barker's excellent book "Voluntary Islam"

Islam and the discovery of freedom

I read the entirety of *"Islam and the Discovery of Freedom"* by Rose Wilder Lane on a direct flight from San Francisco to New Hampshire. I literally cried as she chronicled the great liberty of the past being eclipsed by tyranny. In my heart I found a new love for my friend and teacher Imam Suhaib Webb, whose Islamic literacy class gave me the tools necessary to better grasp the meaning of the commentary by Dr. Imad-ad-Deen Ahmad. Born in 1886, Rose Wilder Lane is regarded as one of the founding mothers of the libertarian movement. Her book The Discovery of Freedom: Man's Struggle Against Authority is said to have been written from beginning to end in "a white heat" and consequently contains numerous historical (but not philosophical) errors. Dissatisfied, and perhaps embarrassed, by these errors, Lane withdrew it from publication, but in her wisdom she devoted a chapter to Islam's contributions to the philosophy of liberty. Now that chapter is available with commentary provided by Dr. Imad-ad-Deen Ahmad of the Minaret of Freedom Institute. He corrects her minor historical and theological errors, but further bolsters her thesis that the golden age of Islamic civilization was the product of its abundant liberty, and its downfall was the result of its decline into tyranny.

Lane begins by summarizing Abraham's message as, *"there is only one God, who has blessed mankind with freewill. They bear accountability for their righteous or evil actions. The pagan gods do not exist, and do not control the affairs of mankind."* She regards this as the first great attempt to liberate mankind from illegitimate authority, and describes history as a struggle between this conviction, that human beings are self-controlling and individually responsible, and attempts by earthly authorities to make themselves into false gods over mankind. She regards Muhammad's message as the second great attempt to establish liberty on Earth. I found her description of the Prophet as a practical, humorous, friendly business executive to be utterly refreshing. In Muhammad's view, according to Lane, priests corrupted the pure message of Abraham, Moses, and Jesus when they assumed authority to control mankind. It was therefore incumbent upon mankind to establish a direct relationship to God without priests. This recognition of mankind as individually volitional beings laid the foundation for what Lane calls the world's first scientific civilization in the modern sense. She writes, *"whenever authority was weak, men opened schools of science,"* because in the Islamic world view there was no distinction between sacred and profane knowledge. All Truth is from God. Lane describes the earliest Islamic universities as marketplaces of knowledge like the bazaars. Men of knowledge came to sell their instruction in open forum, and students were free to wander about listening. When they decided upon a teacher, they met privately to establish a curriculum and agree upon fees. These universities were privately funded and virtually without State regulation. They were regulated by reputation. A teacher's success or failure hinged upon the market demand for the knowledge he sold. If the student was dissatisfied, he simply left to find another teacher, and when he'd had his fill of education, he left school to apply his knowledge. Lane writes, *"Europeans were not able to impose upon that university any tinge of the European belief that minds acquire knowledge, not by actively seeking to know, but by passively being taught whatever Authority decides that they should know."* The result was an explosion of human energy that led to advanced mathematics, medicine, chemistry, astronomy, cosmetics, hygiene, art, and philosophy that appeared like utter magic to medieval Europeans.

Beyond schools, there were also hospitals, libraries, paved roads, and whole water irrigation networks built and maintained by similar private foundations. All institutions and infrastructure that might characterize an advanced civilization were produced without State intervention. Even law was developed by scholars independent of government. Law was not legislated, but discovered the same way that natural scientists discover the laws of physical, chemical, and biological systems. A judge, or qadi, was independent of the State. To keep his reputation for wisdom, he had to find ways to settle disputes that satisfied everyone's sense of justice. No single organization, religious, social, or political, extended over the whole civilization. No monopoly means no State by modern definitions. Lane makes the argument, quite effectively in fact, that through Italy the Muslims gave Europe the enlightenment, and through Spain the Muslims gave Europe the maps, the navigational tools, and the love for freedom that drove them to the New World.

In Muslim Spain, generations of European Christians and Jews experienced freedom of thought and conscience unprecedented anywhere else in Europe. In the century after Granada fell and Spain returned to Catholic rule, the Spaniards were less submissive to government than any other Europeans, and it was during that century that Spaniards explored and conquered the New World. Lane suggests it was the love of freedom learned from the Muslims that drove free-thinking Europeans away from tyranny and across the Atlantic Ocean. Most Muslims fled to Muslim lands, but those who stayed in Spain were forced to convert to Catholicism and came to be called Moriscos.

There was doubt about the sincerity of their conversion when they persisted in their Islamic customs such as reading ... and bathing. The State responded by burning libraries, and prohibiting the Moriscos from bathing secretly in their homes. The Spanish Inquisition began in large part to expose secret Muslims in Spain, and uncover the "*Apostasies and Treasons of the Moriscos.*" In 1602, among the charges against the Moriscos was that they "*commended nothing so much as that liberty of conscience in all matters of religion, which the Turks and all other Mohammedans suffer their subjects to enjoy.*" What the investigation found was that freedom of thought, skepticism of government, and passion for freedom had infected Spaniards who had never been Muslim. So, naturally, those Christians accustomed to this freedom, who could not abide such religious persecution, fled to the New World. According to Lane, Muslims "forgot the God of Abraham" sometime in the 16th century, and rejected the personal responsibility of freedom. Islamic civilization began to resemble the rest of Europe as a static society of controlling authority. But the mantle of liberty had been passed to the Americans directly from the Muslims in Spain. Lane regards the American Revolution as the third and most current attempt to establish a free society on Earth, where political conditions would not hinder mankind's natural inclination toward scientific progress. Many Muslims will speak of the Islamic golden age as an invitation to non-Muslims to challenge their stereotypes of Islam. This is not my aim. I intend to look to this glorious past and imagine what progress we are capable of if only we demand the freedom from tyranny they had in those days. Unfortunately, Lane offers virtually no explanation for why the Muslim world changed. But if we're ever to reclaim the liberty we have lost, it's important that we don't try to manage the symptoms and instead diagnose the disease. It's important that we acknowledge that the success of the past was not achieved by central authority, but by living in conditions where human energy was free from control.

Ninth-Century Muslim Anarchists

I came across an article titled *"Ninth-Century Muslim Anarchists"* by Patricia Crone, scholar of early Islamic history at the Institute for Advanced Study, Princeton, which centers around a discussion that was taking place in Basra in southern Iraq in the 800s. There was a general consensus that the Abbasid Caliphate, which controlled a vast empire from Baghdad, had become corrupt and tyrannical. So the question among the scholars became how the community should respond to a leader who had become *"all too reminiscent of Pharaoh,"* as Crone puts it. This article was originally published in 2000 in the Past & Present journal.

But in light of the Arab Spring, I think it's valuable to pick up the discussion where they left off. The mainstream opinions are broadly categorized as activists and quietists by Crone. The activists held that when a leader lost legitimacy, it was obligatory to stage a violent revolution and install a new legitimate leader. The quietists held that civil war was worse than oppression and it was obligatory to patiently persevere under tyranny. You had to obey the tyrant, or at the most, resist passively. For whatever reason, the quietist position has been and remains the dominant position, even though it contradicts the opinion of Muhammad's companion Abu Bakr, who said upon his inauguration, *"Obey me as long as I obey God and His Prophet. But if I disobey God's command or His Prophet, then no obedience is incumbent upon you."* The quietist position undoubtedly has contributed to the current state of political affairs in Muslim majority countries. Unfettered State power is and always will be expanding State power. There was a third category of solutions they were exploring that Crone calls "anarchist." Most of these were what Crone calls "reluctant anarchists," in that they believed that the society could function without the Caliph.

For them, anarchism was not an ideal they hoped to achieve, but the acknowledgment that the ideal, the Medina Caliphate, was lost, and could not be restored. They proposed a kind of evolutionary anarchism. They made no proposal to abolish private property, except to say that the illegitimacy of the ruler spoiled the validity of titles to property, presumably those granted by the ruler. This may be similar to the way some modern libertarians view eminent domain, corporate title, and intellectual property as invalid. Predominantly it was factions among the Mu'tazilites, the Kharijites, and the Sufis who proposed that if leaders kept turning into tyrants, perhaps they'd be better off without leaders at all.

Essentially they argued that the Caliph must be agreed upon by the entire community, either unanimously or by consensus, and that without this, no legitimate Caliph could exist. It was widely accepted that God did not impose obligations that were impossible to fulfill, so it was reasoned that there was no obligation to establish a legitimate Caliph, although hardly any of them denied the possibility of one emerging in the future. But in the meantime alternatives had to be explored. Some pointed out that the Bedouins had got along fine without rulers.

Crone writes, *"anarchists were clearly drawing on the tribal tradition which lies behind all early Islamic political thought of the type which may be loosely identified as libertarian."* Crone didn't specify this in the article, but this view of the Caliphate is consistent with the hadith in which the Prophet informed us that after him would be leaders who followed his example, then there would be kings, and then there would be tyrants. If you accept this hadith, it's clear that we have progressed from Caliphs to kings, and hard to argue we haven't progressed from kings to tyrants.

Viewed this way, any attempt to reestablish the Caliphate by force could only result in further tyranny. Their specific reasons for arguing against the Caliphate is not particularly relevant to us today, as there has not been a Caliphate, legitimate of otherwise, since the collapse of the Ottoman Empire. The reality for us is that this is less an intellectual exercise than a practical necessity, especially in light of the tenuous grip the current tyrannies hold over their people.

Their proposed solutions of the "reluctant anarchists" ranged from a radical decentralization of public authority to a complete dissolution of public authority. A subset of proposals involved replacing the Caliph with elected officials, the argument being that if you polled enough people, you minimized the danger of bias and collusion that had become the signature of the Caliphate. These proposals could be called "minarchist" in modern parlance. They proposed that people could elect trustworthy and learned leaders within their local communities, the argument being that there could never be unanimous agreement upon one leader of the Muslims, and one could not assess the quality of candidates at great distances.

These leaders could either be completely independent of one another, or they could be joined together in a federation, the argument being that independent leaders would forever be fighting with their neighbors. This is strikingly reminiscent of the federalist vs. anti-federalist debate that took place in the American colonies 1,000 years later. Some minarchists viewed these elected officials as temporary, only remaining in office when legal disputes arose, or when an enemy invaded. When the problem was resolved they would lose their positions, much as an imam does when he has finished leading prayer, and society could return to statelessness. This is very similar to the stateless judicial system in Somalia today, which we will discuss next. Admittedly the minarchist proposals were not really anarchist. They advocated abolishing the form of government to which they had grown accustomed and replacing it with systems with far more public participation. Most of them were proposing new forms of government for which they had no historical precedent. But there were still some who were true anarchists in that they wanted a complete dissolution of public authority. Some argued that a sufficiently moral society would have no need for authority, while others argued that because society was not sufficiently moral, they couldn't have a legitimate authority. Either way, they believed that the welfare of society would be best if people were only left alone. The most prominent group calling for the complete abolition of the State was a minority sect called the Najdiyya. They argued that so long as there was not sufficient agreement to establish a legitimate Caliph, there could never be enough to establish law at all. Even the consensus of scholars could not be a source of law in a community where no unified consensus existed anyway. To the Najdiyya every individual was responsible for his own salvation, and entitled to his own legal interpretations through independent reasoning (ijtihad). Indeed, any intellectual tradition must be built on this foundation, because in order to persuade others to adopt it, you must first appeal to their independent reasoning.

The Najdiyya not only demanded political independence, but complete intellectual independence, because believers were, as the Prophet said, "like the teeth of a comb," and therefore should have no master but God himself. Divine law could be conceived of as the natural law, available to all mankind, like fingerprints in the clay of Adam. Crone calls this "*radical libertarianism,*" and as far as I can tell, it is one of the first appearances of it in history. None of the anarchists or minarchists explained how to put their proposals into practice while the State still existed. They merely speculated, leaving it to future generations to implement their radical reform. We may be those generations. None of them proposed fomenting rebellion, happy to enjoy the comforts the State provided its intellectuals. Only the Sufis avoided material comforts, but their solution was simply to transcend politics and seek meaning in other pursuits, not to revolt. However, in 817 anarchy was foisted upon them when the government in Baghdad collapsed. A civil war had ousted the previous Caliph and the influence of the new Caliph hadn't been established yet. Chaos ensued, and the public responded, as many would have predicted, by forming a vigilante group to protect private property, maintain commerce, and allow the meek to move freely through Baghdad. This is exactly the kind of spontaneous order we saw in Egypt when police in plainclothes picked fights and looted stores. Civilians self-organized into neighborhood watch programs to protect each other. We see now what they saw then: in the absence of public authority there is a natural emergence of order out of chaos without central planning. The Muslim anarchists of the ninth century concluded, as many have in the modern world, *that when people are forced to rely on themselves, they discover talents they did not know they had.*

Chapter 14- Intersections of Buddhism and Anarchism

This chapter will focus on the philosophy of Buddhism, specifically Zen, and Anarchy, specifically Agorism. Zen is the Japanese pronunciation for Chan or Dhyana, which translates roughly to "meditation". It is also the name for the school of Mahayana Buddhism that began in China and spread to the south and east around the 6th century of the current era.

Although certain sects of Buddhism have promoted obedience and been used as state religion, Zen Buddhism was actually a rejection of certain ritualized Buddhist practices and philosophy that had become more rigid since the death of the Buddha, Siddhartha Gautama.

Siddhartha is believed to have been born a prince in the subcontinent of India about five centuries before the current era. His parents did their best to shelter him. However, the story says that at age twenty-nine, Siddhartha made several trips outside of his pampered palace and witnessed human suffering for the first time in his life in the form of a sick elderly man, and a dead body. Siddhartha decided to abandon his privileged life and begin a spiritual quest.

After trying out extremes of deep, dedicated meditation and fasting to the point of starvation, the former prince discovered The Middle Way, a path of balance and moderation. At age thirty-five, while meditating under the Bodhi tree, he achieved enlightenment as he touched the Earth, declaring his victory over Mara, a demon that represents temptation. From then until the time of his death in his eighties, The Buddha taught his philosophy of compassion, non-violence, meditation and non-attachment.

Around twelve centuries after the Buddha's life, an Indian monk named Bodhidharma was credited with bringing Buddhism to China and popularizing the importance of Zazen, or sitting meditation. He taught that the path to enlightenment would not come from reciting the Buddha's words or lighting a certain amount of candles, but rather by doing what the Buddha was doing when he achieved enlightenment - meditating.

The Buddha's victory over Mara underneath the Bodhi tree is the reason Zen stresses the importance of Zazen. Through Zazen we better understand the nature of reality as we achieve self-realization by recognizing the truth that there is nothing but the present moment.

Zen and the Agora: Anarchy, Agora, Action and Awareness

As we noted earlier, Agorism is the branch of Anarchy that focuses on self-sufficiency, the idea of counter economics, black and grey markets and on creating alternatives to state institutions. Our desire for Anarchy comes from a desire for collective liberation. Our interest in Agorism comes from a demand for actions that create solutions in this life in attempt to create a better world.

While Agorism calls for action in the physical realm by creating alternative currencies, self-sufficiency, and barter networks, Zen calls for action in the mental realm. Zen is the action of the mind. In Zen, the greatest action you can take is to sit, still your mind, and be with yourself. You must silence the noise and detach. It is about connecting with your mind and recognizing the ultimate truth of reality and freedom beyond words.

Both these philosophies call for action. One calls for action in the physical world, the other in the internal world, but both are about taking action. Meditation is a completely personal and direct experience. It "requires" letting go of fears, insecurities, and ego. Whatever you find in your own mind – nobody can take that away from you. In terms of anarchy, we see meditation as our direct connection to being sovereign, free humans with no authority over us. We are not pretending that this (or anything in this book) is a one size fits all solution, because obviously those don't work. Rather, we are providing another option– what we believe is a further evolvement of Anarchism.

In the *New Libertarian Manifesto*, the first book to introduce Agorism,

Samuel Konkin III writes, *"there is no one way, one straight line graph to liberty to be sure, but there is a family of graphs that will take the libertarian to his goal of a free society and that space can be described."* We believe another solution is having a sense of spirituality and an understanding of self-reflection, coupled with a philosophical understanding of anarchy and the role of government.

It is not enough to simply understand the nature of government and the immorality of force. If we do not learn about ourselves and conquer our inner demons in attempt to get to the root causes of statism, statism will live on. We may be able to beat the current government, but until we explore the root of the issue, a new type of statism will exist every couple hundred years or so.

Konkin continues, "*a lot more than statism would need to be eliminated from individual consciousness for this society to exist. Most damaging of all to this perfectly free society is its lack of a mechanism of correction. All it takes is a handful of practitioners of coercion who enjoy their ill-gotten plunder in enough company to sustain them – and freedom is dead. Even if all are living free, one "bite of the apple," one throwback, reading old history or rediscovering evil on his own, will "unfree" the perfect society,*" (page 25)

It will take more than the elimination of Statism to create a free society. We can spread the ideas of liberty, anarchy, self-rule, an understanding the immorality of force and the like, but until we as individuals deeply examine our own inconsistencies, we are doomed to repeat the same mistakes and create a new form of Statism. Humanity must pursue an understanding of the self and the motivation behind violence, theft, and fear. If free people continue to be bound by fear, we will keep creating the same situation.

In Buddhism, the endless cycle of life and death, which students of the Middle Path seek to end, is known as Samsara. Until you gain a level of balance and tacit awareness through meditation, chanting, prayer or ritual (depending on the sect of Buddhism) you will continue the cycle of Samsara. As a species we find ourselves stuck in State Samsara, an endless cycle of attempting to fix the world and manage humanity's problems by allowing a small group to maintain a monopoly on force and violence. It doesn't work. We will continue this cycle until every individual makes a choice to go within and stop feeding the state.

When Konkin introduced Agorism, he also introduced the three A's. These include the Agora, Anarchy and Action. "Agora", meaning the marketplace, the exchange - humans interacting freely without interference. "Anarchy" or self-rule, and "Action", or what's needed to move these things forward. Equally powerful as the three A's are the Buddhist sentiments of wisdom, compassion and action.

If you have wisdom, you possess knowledge and know how to use it. You have a solid understanding of the physical world around you. With wisdom but no compassion for your fellow human being you are all mind and no heart. However if you are all compassion, being lead solely by your heart and possessing no wisdom, then you might find yourself being taken advantage of and lead astray. Even if you have wisdom and compassion for yourself and the community around you, nothing gets done without action. It is with this in mind that we propose a fourth A for the spiritual Agorist.

We believe that "Awareness" should be a part of the Agorist path– Awareness of self, so you can better know yourself and better "rule" yourself. How can we know what freedom means to us if we do not know ourselves? This is also considered mindful awareness or mindfulness– Mindfulness with our interactions with the community, in the market and in our actions.

When we apply the same understanding and awareness to our individual paths and our place in the universe, we are furthering our understanding of what it truly means to be free. It is time for us to slow down, be conscious and become more aware of our own thoughts, words and actions. From this balanced standpoint we can begin to build alternative institutions that will rival the state and allow freedom to flourish.

Consistency from Samuel Konkin III to Siddhartha Gautama

Throughout our lives we encounter individuals who profess certain ideas or principles, whether political or otherwise, yet display behavior quite the opposite of their words. After repeatedly witnessing such hypocrisy, one learns not to trust the words of such a person. If we cannot be held accountable for our actions and words, why bother taking anyone seriously?

In the "*New Libertarian Manifesto*", Samuel Konkin III speaks of the importance of consistency. He writes:

"The basic principle which leads a libertarian from statism to his free society is the same which the founders of libertarianism used to discover the theory itself. That principle is consistency. Thus, the consistent application of the theory of libertarianism to every action the individual libertarian takes creates the libertarian society.

Many thinkers have expressed the need for consistency between means and ends and not all were libertarians. Ironically, many statists have claimed inconsistency between laudable ends and contemptible means; yet when their true ends of greater power and oppression were understood, their means are found to be quite consistent. It is part of the statist mystique to confuse the necessity of ends-means consistency; it is thus the most crucial activity of the libertarian theorist to expose inconsistencies," (Page 23).

Konkin understood the importance of consistency when it comes to libertarian/anarchist philosophy and we can take it even further. Remove the strictly libertarian mindset from the sentences and we see they remain applicable to any individual regardless of their political or philosophical association.

"The application of consistency to every action the individual takes creates a more consistent society."

Obviously, as Konkin states, Statists are quite inconsistent as well. They may claim to stand for certain principles, yet their actions show their true nature and intentions. One can assume the Statists in power are either completely unaware of their actions, or are, in fact, total and complete liars.

Siddhartha Gautama also spoke about the importance of consistency: The Buddha believed mindfulness and self-awareness were the two keys to eliminating suffering. He believed one could attain a new understanding of self and move past the dualistic understanding of reality by turning the focus inside and meditating.

With a consistent application of compassion and self-reflection, the Buddhist sees a way to free the people from themselves and thus create a more free society. We see the importance of consistency in this quote attributed to the Buddha:

"Mind precedes all mental states. Mind is their chief; they are all mind-wrought. If with a pure mind a person speaks or acts happiness follows him like his never-departing shadow," ("The Pairs", Dhammapada,).

What you create in thought form becomes your words. After repeatedly listening to your words, your actions begin to reflect your thinking. So if you are of the Statist mindset, you speak from a Statist perspective and your actions and character reflect your Statist position. On the other hand if you are pursuing ideas of compassion, the Non-Aggression Principle, self-rule and reflection, it follows that your thoughts, words and actions will reflect the same.

This is in line with Voluntaryist philosophy. Author Albert Jay Nock said it best in his book *Memoirs of a Superfluous Man – "Ages of experience testify that the only way society can be improved is by the individualist method...that is, the method of each 'one' doing his very best to improve 'one'. Voluntaryists believe that this is the quiet, peaceful, patient way of changing society because it concentrates on bettering the character of men and women as individuals. The voluntaryist hope is that as the individual units change, the improvement of society will take care of itself. In other words, "if one take care of the means, the end will take care of itself,"* .

Once again the ideas of introspection and self-governance align. We see great value in a path that includes an autonomous, sovereign practice of Zen meditation, compassion and non-violence that also respects the principles of self-governance and self-determination.

Chapter 15 - Intersections of Taoism and Anarchism

Taoism is an ancient Chinese tradition which emphasizes living in harmony with what is referred to as Tao. The term Tao means "way", "path" or "principle". It is a concept found in Chinese philosophies and religions. However, in Taoism, the Tao is believed to be both the source and the force behind everything that exists.

Although Taoism drew its cosmological philosophy from the School of Yin Yang, the Tao Te Ching by early Chinese philosopher Lao-tzu is considered by many to be its primary source. Tao Te Ching roughly translates to, *The Book of The Natural Way and of Natural Virtues.*

Written around 600 years before the current era, the Tao Te Ching presents a model of *Wu-Wei*, action without action, or non-action. Wu-Wei is not the promotion of absence of action, but the state of being in harmony with the nature of things, or Tao. Lao-tzu has been recognized as one of the earliest known anti-authoritarian thinkers. He espoused a very individualist philosophy, which saw social institutions as a hindrance, not a benefit for human beings. Lao-tzu's writings explored the errors of prohibitions and government regulation many centuries before anyone else was challenging these concepts.

In Chapter 57 of the Tao Te Ching, Lao-Tzu writes:

"If you want to be a great leader, you must learn to follow the Tao. Stop trying to control.

Let go of fixed plans and concepts, and the world will govern itself. The more prohibitions you have, the less virtuous people will be. The more weapons you have, the less secure people will be. The more subsidies you have, the less self-reliant people will be. Therefore the Master says:

I let go of the law, and people become honest. I let go of economics, and people become prosperous. I let go of religion, and people become serene. I let go of all desire for the common good, and the good becomes common as grass."

In Chapter 75, Lao-Tzu comments on the importance of self-governance:

"When taxes are too high, people go hungry. When government is too intrusive, people lose their spirit. Act for the peoples benefit. Trust them; leave them alone."

In Chapter 31, Lao-Tzu references the principles of non-aggression and non- violence.

"Weapons are the tools of violence; all decent men detest them.
Weapons are the tools of fear; a decent man will avoid them except in the direst necessity and, if compelled, will use them only with the utmost restraint. Peace is his highest value.
If the peace has been shattered, how can he be content?
His enemies are not demons, but human beings like himself.
He doesn't wish them personal harm. Nor does he rejoice in victory.
How could he rejoice in victory and delight in the slaughter of men?"

Two centuries after Lao-tzu' came philosopher Chuang-tzu, who took the teachings of his predecessor a step further. His writings became so popular that his intellectual services were sought far and wide, even among the aristocracy and monarchy. Eventually, Chuang-tzu received an offer from King Wei of the Ch'u kingdom to serve as his chief minister of state. Chuang-tzu passionately refused his offer and gave the following statement in response:

"A thousand ounces of gold is indeed a great reward, and the office of chief minister is truly an elevated position. But have you, sir, not seen the sacrificial ox awaiting the sacrifices at the royal shrine of state? It is well cared for and fed for a few years, caparisoned with rich brocades, so that it will be ready to be led into the Great Temple. At that moment, even though it would gladly change places with any solitary pig, can it do so? So, quick and be off with you! Don't sully me, I would rather roam and idle about in a muddy ditch, at my own amusement, than to be put under the restraints that the ruler would impose. I will never take any official service, and thereby I will satisfy my own purposes," (The Complete Works of Chuang Tzu).

Chuang-tzu put forward many bold anti-state positions in his writing, including the following statements, sourced by Murray Rothbard in his work *Concepts of the Role of Intellectuals in Social Change Toward Laissez Faire*:

"There has never been such a thing as letting mankind alone; there has never been such a thing as governing mankind with success. Letting alone springs from fear lest men's natural dispositions be perverted and their virtue left aside. But if their natural dispositions be not perverted nor their virtue laid aside, what room is there left for government?"

He has also been quoted as saying that the world *"does not need governing; in fact it should not be governed."*

In the nineteenth and twentieth centuries, philosophers like Proudhon and Hayek were pioneering the concept of *"spontaneous order"*, but even earlier, the Taoist teachings of Lao-Tzu and Chuang-tzu taught that,

"Good order results spontaneously when things are let alone." This balanced perspective of self-reflection and self-governance is a key aspect of both Anarchism and Taoism. Despite criticism from some scholars who believe that Taoism was a tool for the elite to pacify the peasant class, the philosophy is completely consistent with the ideas of withdrawing from the State and working with the natural flow of the world. Rather than solely fighting external battles against State powers, the lesson is to follow the Tao, the natural way. This natural state of humanity is, of course, a path that lacks force and coercion as imposed by state institutions.

In his book, *Demanding the Impossible: A History of Anarchism*, Peter Marshall writes:

"It is impossible to appreciate the ethics and politics of Taoism without an understanding of its philosophy of nature. The Tao te ching celebrates the Tao, or way, of nature and describes how the wise person should follow it. The Taoist conception of nature is based on the ancient Chinese principles of yin and yang, two opposite but complementary forces in the cosmos which constitute ch'i (matter-energy) of which all beings and phenomena are formed. Yin is the supreme feminine power, characterized by darkness, cold, and receptivity and associated with the moon; yang is the masculine counterpart of brightness, warmth, and activity, and is

identified with the sun. Both forces are at work within men and women as well as in all things," (page 54).

Taoism teaches that individuals who pursue balance with nature will be happy, free people who do not wish to be oppressed or oppress others. Instead, students of the Tao find themselves content to walk their own path in harmony with the external world and to spread the gospel of the Tao.

(All quotations from the Tao te Ching are reprinted from Stephen Mitchell's translation.)

Chapter 16 - Zomia and the Art Of Not Being Governed

Throughout this book we have suggested that people of various cultures, ethnicities, religions and philosophical backgrounds can share the same geography in relative peace without a government for long periods of time. This is no fairy tale or utopian pipe dream, but a documented historical fact.

Until recently, a mountainous region of Southeast Asia the size of Europe was completely stateless. In fact, the area was almost entirely inhabited by anarchists who had fled into the mountains to escape the reaches of various governments. Naturally, there was no official name or flag for this area, but it has been thoroughly studied and in 2002, European historian Willem van Schendel of the University of Amsterdam named the region *Zomia*. In 2009, Yale Professor James C. Scott expanded on the study of the region with his book *The Art of Not Being Governed: An Anarchist History of Upland Southeast Asia.*

Zomia was an area of around 2.5 million square kilometers, spanning from the central highlands of Vietnam to northeastern India, covering five Southeast nations including Vietnam, Cambodia, Laos, Thailand, and Burma. The area contained around one hundred million minority peoples. It was not an actual state, but a collection of many peoples and regions mainly living in the hills and mountainous regions that were largely unwanted or inaccessible to the State. Scott's argument is that these widely varied peoples came together to trade among each other and developed customs and practices that were inherently anti-state. As evidenced by their agriculture, politics and spirituality, they sought to live in ways that were not congruent with Statism. In the preface to The Art of Not Being Governed, Scott writes, *"these people's livelihoods, social organization, ideologies and oral cultures can be read as strategic positionings designed to keep the state at arms length."*

Rather than seeing humanity as having evolved towards the conveniences of the modern state, he argues that until recently, humans organized through self-governing kinship units that would cooperate in hunting, fighting, trading and peacemaking. *"In other words, living in the absence of state structures has been the standard of the human condition,"* (*The Art of Not Being Governed*, page 3). Instead, he argues, we should recognize that many people purposefully live and operate outside of the state for as long as possible.

"Their subsistence routines, their social organization, their physical dispersal, and many elements of their culture, far from being the archaic traits of a people left behind, are purposefully crafted both to thwart incorporations into nearby states and to minimize the likelihood that statelike concentrations of power will arise among them. State evasion and state prevention permeate their experiences and, often, their ideology as well," (page 8).

The establishment of villages allowed the state to encourage the peasantry to remain sedentary, and thus, able to be taxed and brought into the fold of State control and influence. In Zomia, attempts to assimilate non-state communities were less about development and economic progress than they were about ensuring that economic activity in these communities was taxable and confiscatable if needed. This highlights the importance of building counter-institutions through Agorism. As Scott mentions, *"the main, long-run threat of the ungoverned periphery, however, was that it represented a constant temptation, a constant alternative to life within the state,"* (page 6).

Once free communities are established and thriving outside of the State, those living under state rule will be quick to consider the alternative. Scott also notes that the myth of state powers being able to save peasants from the clutches of barbarians is largely false. He argues that refugees of the State were quite common as people recognized that life under a State might mean taxes, conscription in wars, forced labor and servitude. This cycle of state-making and state-unmaking created zones of refuge, or "shatter zones", where those escaping the clutches of the State came together to form complex groupings of various ethnicities and family units. This complexity, along with "relative geographical inaccessibility", were common characteristics of these shatter zones. Groups seeking to escape the State would form partnerships and reside in areas that growing government influence could not reach.

When discussing the differences between the valleys of the state and the mountainous regions that make up Zomia, Scott remarks, *"The hills, unlike the valleys, have paid neither taxes to monarchs nor regular tithes to a permanent religious establishment. They have constituted a relatively free, stateless population of foragers and hill farmers,"* (page 19).

Zomia has been the site of indigenous struggles, secessionist movements and armed opposition movements. The spiritual beliefs of Zomia often leaned towards Animism, a rather decentralized viewpoint that sees God in all objects, rather than exclusively in spiritual traditions and religions that have been used to centralize the people, such as Theravada Buddhism. In the same way Native Americans saw their belief systems threatened or completely extinguished by Christian missionaries, residents of Zomia faced similar threats from the Buddhist orthodoxy that sought to ban local deities and practices. Scott believes the animist practices and other forms of belief outside the accepted canon *"represent zones of resistant difference, dissent, and, at the very least, failures of incorporation and domestication by state-promoted religion,"* (page 300).

Zomia was not the only stateless region throughout history. Prior to the advent of modern travel and technology, many cultures of many lands found freedom living in a wide variety of decentralized, anarchist societies that were outside the city walls and outside the reaches of the empires. It has been written in the history books that these people were savages and primitives who had no knowledge or contact with the so-called "civilized" world. However, in the case of Zomia and other breakaway cultures, we see that these societies were well aware of the empires and wanted nothing to do with them.

The struggles of American Indians best exemplify this concept. Far from the fairy tale Thanksgiving, the history of the relations between the United States government and the Indigenous peoples of North America has been filled with violence and war. American Indians recognized that the colonizers were not after cooperation and partnership, but were using their doctrine of Manifest Destiny to take what they wanted from whomever they wanted. For five hundred years governments of the world have failed to recognize the sovereignty and autonomy of indigenous communities.

George E. Tinker, Professor of American Indian Cultures and Religious Traditions at Iliff School of Theology and a member of the Osage Nation, believes it is this failure that has caused so much harm to indigenous peoples who do not wish to assimilate. In his book *Spirit and Resistance: Political Theology and American Indian Liberation*, Tinker writes,

"Namely, the political and economic bias in the international discourse is to recognize only states as the fundamental actors in the international political discourse. As such, the natural national identities that make up indigenous peoples' communities are seen today as merely ethnic minorities within state structures, who may have individual rights but do not have any distinct set of community or cultural right as an independent people, " (page 7).

Tinker believes the growing state could not accept Indians living amongst themselves; it needed them to join the coming status quo. The colonizers had a burning desire to "civilize" the natives. *"The result was the consistent imposition of european cultural values, norms, societal structures, and technologies on peoples who had lived remarkably well with their own values, norms, structures, and technologies for some thousands of years, "* (page 10).

This trend continues today in the form of "sustainable development" projects that only further colonize and damage indigenous communities. Whether we are speaking of those indigenous to the North American landmass or Zomia, there is a consistent history of oppression by states and refusal to accept the autonomy of these groups. (*For further reading on indigenous communities that operated in an essentially stateless fashion read Pierre Clastres' Society Against the State.*) However, indigenous communities are not the only populations oppressed by the state.

Despite the seeming normalcy and convenience of living under the control of a state, there is a much freer world waiting outside the imagined boundaries of state institutions. Learning that freedom truly begins within is a huge lesson we hope to impart. We believe that once we work to know ourselves more deeply and begin the process of healing on an individual level, the ideas of living in cooperative, autonomous Panarchist communities built around the ideas of mutual-aid, non-aggression, voluntaryism and mindfulness, will become much more appealing. In fact, as these ideas grow they seem so obvious that it makes us wonder– what has taken humanity so long? As usual, all things happen in the time and space they are supposed to.

We see much hope in the growing interest in freedom, Anarchy, self-reflection and cooperation. Together we are creating a paradigm shift that will allow our planet to heal and evolve towards a more peaceful, free, awakened state of being. We thank you for being a part of this journey.

Remember, if you can see this, you are The Conscious Resistance.

UPDATE 8/31/15:

Since the release of this book in April 2015 we have made several edits to fix grammar and spacing issues, as well as to further elaborate a few of our points. We plan to continue updating the book in future editions.

We have also realized that this book is the first in a trilogy we are writing. The second book, tentatively titled "Finding Freedom in an Age of Confusion", will be a collection of essays which will delve more deeply into some of the ideas presented within this book.

The third book will dig further into implementing Agorist strategies, engaging in counter-economics, and building counter-institutions. Think of it as a "How to Escape the Matrix" type of book.

We look forward to sharing more of our words and ideas with you. Thanks for the support.

- Derrick Broze and John Vibes

UPDATE 2/8/17:

We are close to releasing book 3, Manifesto of the Free Humans, and have finally released the audiobook! We hope you enjoy the upcoming book and ideas! See you on the road!

- John and Derrick

Our Journeys: About the Authors:

John Vibes

Since as far back as I can remember I largely rejected the cultural traditions that I was born into, because they seemed unnatural, irrational and oppressive. School was difficult because even from a young age I refused to conform and somehow understood that I wasn't going to learn anything of value in school. Most of my teachers in elementary school resented me because I would bring in books on topics that I was interested in and I would read them to myself while the class was going over their indoctrinating lesson. By the time high school came around I was so sick of the whole thing that I spent my class time sleeping, drinking and doing drugs, and from time to time I would still read. The oppressive nature of the school system only pushed me to hold greater resentment against authority and mainstream society. Unfortunately, that resentment pushed me toward some naive conclusions.

Although I had my suspicions about society and the status quo, I was still heavily conditioned by media and operating on a fairly low level of consciousness. I was still seeing the world in black and white terms and was pushed towards ideas like Satanism and Communism, because I was so turned off with the typical mainstream culture that I was subject to, that I just ran in the total opposite direction for solutions. Like many of the pitfalls I encountered, this was a necessary adventure along my path, and vital to my learning experience. Those interests led me to a wide variety of philosophical studies, but nothing would really make sense to me until many years later when I had enough information to get a clear picture of how things really worked. Most of my adolescence was filled with misplaced angst and overindulgence, which I hear is fairly typical. Regular drug tests pushed me towards heavy alcohol and pharmaceutical use, so although I was using psychedelics and researching philosophy I was still very clouded because of the mind numbing chemicals that I was putting into my body and the media that I surrounded myself with. Through those years I was faced with many synchronistic situations that slowly led me toward a more conscious lifestyle and informed perspective, but it would be many years before I broke free from the state of sleep that I was in.

There is no doubt that every single one of us has our whole perception of reality crafted by our environment and the things we experience, I'm obviously no different. Like most of the people on the planet I was born into a life of serfdom and grew up being constantly reminded about the struggles and obstacles that came along with financial slavery. Many times I was shown firsthand the senseless violence of war and the threatening oppression of the legal system, as you can tell my story is not unique, almost anyone can relate. The issues that have impacted my life and the ones I discuss in this book affect everyone, they are not limited to my experience.

Things did begin to get a little bit out of the ordinary when I started working at a funeral home at the age of 17. Looking back it's hard to imagine that I was drawn to that kind of profession, but at the time I was a very confused person. I ended up spending about 6 years as an apprentice mortician and those were quite possibly the most turbulent times of my life. I'm sure that the late teen to young adult phase is no cakewalk for anyone, but my job and my drinking problem seemed to at least keep things interesting.

They say you should never regret anything, and for the most part I agree, but if I could take back anything I wouldn't have let my drinking get so out of hand. At the time I was very ignorant, and underestimated the toxicity of alcohol due to its cultural acceptance. I was left with health problems that I'm still trying to sort out today. I was never an aggressive drunk, but that doesn't mean that I wasn't an extremely stupid drunk that caused a lot of trouble for myself and other people. Believe it or not it would take an enlightening shamanic experience to make me realize that I was destroying my body and that I should probably phase out my alcohol use. After 7 years of drinking hard liquor on a daily basis it was a lot easier to quit then I ever thought it would be, and with every day that passed I became more conscious of what was going on around me.

Due to my own personal experience and my earlier research into philosophy I was always untrusting of power, government, war, finance, religion and authority in general, but I didn't have enough of the specific background information to fully understand the true nature of our reality. I had a very limited knowledge of occult history for most of my life and was heavily sedated by chemicals and cultural assumptions that I greatly underestimated due to my ignorance. That all began to change when my physical and mental health started to deteriorate from alcohol abuse, heavy smoking and extremely poor eating habits. I was partying constantly because I was so disgusted with society and the life that seemed to lie before me, because it just seemed so confusing and backwards. I saw a world consumed with greed, violence, pain and misunderstanding for no apparent reason. This wasn't the kind of world I wanted to live in. I didn't want anyone to be subject to violence and I didn't approve of the status quo, but I was so convinced that this was the only world that was possible that I made no attempt to do anything about it and led a hedonistic lifestyle in order to fill a void in my soul.

During that period I was immersed in the heavy metal circuit in Baltimore and although mostly everyone was distracted by sex, drugs n rock n roll, I synchronistically met some activists and artists who were using the scene as a social platform. My new friends and acquaintances taught me all sorts of new information about the monetary system, social engineering and specifically the new world order. After putting a few tidbits together with the research I had done in the past, light bulbs went off all over the place in my head and I began to scour the internet for more information. There I found piles of documented evidence that supported what I knew all along but had no clue how to put into words. Eventually after enough research, it became easier to find the words and I could accurately explain to myself and others why I disapproved of the status quo and exactly who was responsible for perpetuating it.

Unfortunately, even with my newfound knowledge I was still making poor decisions and still had a very negative outlook. My whole worldview was still heavily conditioned by years of media, schooling, and cultural norms. I was still looking at things in a very nihilistic way, where I had no understanding of the higher spiritual levels that existed or the unbelievable things that could be achieved through love and human cooperation. I really hate to be cliché here, but I was to learn all of this at my first hippy festival. I'm going to spare the names, dates and places out of respect for the promoters, but ill share the basics of what happened. This event was something that I had never experienced before and I had no clue what to expect. It ended up being a whole weekend almost completely removed from the mainstream American culture which had held me prisoner for most of my life.

My many adventures and realizations over that weekend would have a huge impact on my future path and encouraged me to delve deeper into the counter culture. After the enlightening weekend I had at that event. I spent the rest of the summer touring similar festivals on the east coast, seeking to clock more time outside of the mainstream culture and return once again down the rabbit hole. That summer my travels brought me to an outdoor rave that was on the water. That was probably one of the best parties I had ever been to, until around 3am when fire trucks, cop cars and other emergency vehicles began to surround the event. Things became very frantic at that point and I decided that I should leave the area where everyone had assembled and find another way out. Just before the area was raided I saw a fishing boat and began to shout to them for help and they came ashore to see what was going on. I offered them 20 dollars to take me and my friends out of harm's way toward where we had parked our car, and luckily the agreed to help us. That certainly wasn't my first close call with the Gestapo that summer.

After a few of these encounters I came to realize that the counter culture truly was outlawed in this Orwellian society I had come to find myself in. I always had a deep suspicion of authority, but now that I had the proper information and witnessed this peaceful culture being demonized by those authoritarian forces, I understood the reality of how our "civilization" operates.

In addition to the personal realizations that came to me at that show I had also made connections which would eventually help me establish myself as a rave promoter. At one of these events I met a promoter from Philly who said he hosted parties at a place called "Gods Basement" and that I should check it out sometime. If it wasn't for that synchronistic random encounter it is highly possible that I never would have wrote this book, thrown a single rave or even met my wife. Without Gods Basement and the time I spent there I can't even begin to imagine what my life would be like today. While I had been to some club and underground events in the past, Gods Basement was my official introduction into the underground rave scene.

When I started partying at Gods Basement, I was still in that part of my life where I was drinking on a daily basis and working at a funeral home in Baltimore. Nearly every day after work I would stop at local bars to kill time before traffic died down and most times I ended up at a place called The Black Hole. Eventually I took on a second job there working the door during rock and hip hop shows to make some extra money. Eventually, The Black Hole began getting involved in raves after a friend of mine made a suggestion to the owner. I helped book and promote a few shows there when things were starting up but was always helping other crews, doing my own shows never really crossed my mind at that point. After a while I began to spend most of my time in Philly and New York networking and promoting for shows at Gods Basement and the The Black Hole, with my wife Kali. At the time we had just recently met, but now we are happily married and I don't know what I would do without her.

Gods Basement was one of the main party spots on the east coast when I began promoting, and The Black Hole was still getting itself established and building its base crowd. Gods Basement is still to this day one of the most awesome venues I have ever been to, and I feel extremely lucky for the time I was able to spend there. As they say though, all good things must come to an end. When Gods Basement came under fire I learned just how corrupt and one sided the media is first hand. At the time I was familiar with media bias but I was still under the impression that the talking heads on the news were just mistaken with good intentions. However, as I would learn, the media consistently and deliberately constructs lies, falsifies reports and intentionally spins stories in order to uphold the status quo.

I'll be the first one to admit that wild things happen at raves, but they still offer a much safer and more peaceful environment than the average rock or hip hop concert that is advertised on mainstream television and radio.

Gods Basement was eventually closed after an ignorant and close minded mother who didn't want her 18 year old child going to the events, reported the underground venue to the local news. Instead of playing an active role in her child's life and attempting to understand what was going on in her child's mind, this parent decided to force her will onto an entire culture.

With her face and voice disguised, she appeared on the news calling for the shutdown of Gods Basement. This bigoted testimony was presented with fake video footage of kids doing various drugs, but long time patrons of Gods Basement could see that the clips which showed this were not even filmed at that venue. After the initial story ran, the NBC news channel received so much feedback defending rave culture that they were forced to run a second story to apparently show the other side of the argument.

As expected, that second segment was a total whitewash, where all legitimate complaints about the hit piece from the day before were mocked and marginalized, leaving the viewer with a skewed version of events. The fact that the promotion crews involved with the venue ran regular charity events and gave back to the community was completely left out of the reports and when it was time for the crew to make a statement their words were distorted and put in a context that made us look careless and unintelligent. The lies and attacks from the media eventually did result in the downfall of Gods Basement. When things got too crazy in Philly, I returned to Baltimore with a new direction and new connections that I developed working as a street promoter for Tru Skool Productions, the crew that ran Gods Basement.

By spring of 2008 I began to start thinking about doing my own shows because there were some elements that I had witnessed in the parties up north, which were lacking from the events in Baltimore and DC. Then shows up north had a more underground feel, with themes, hard dance music and decorations, whereas the parties in my area were club events, not raves. So I approached the The Black Hole with my plan and by June of that year I began hosting my own underground themed events under Good Vibes Promotions. The name was just something that came naturally to me, almost at the same time that I had decided to start a crew. From the first show on things were great, the parties were awesome, crowds came out of nowhere and packed the place every month, things were looking very promising. The only problem we really had was that the venue was in a residential area and we got harassed by the cops on a pretty regular basis. The place never backed down though and launched their own lawsuits on the police department armed with video evidence and countless eyewitnesses on their side, including myself. Unfortunately, years later the police launched a full scale raid and shut down the business, bringing an era to an end and putting many nonviolent human beings in cages. This situation was of course one of the many times in which I experienced the corruption of the legal system first hand.

In the beginning, I knew I enjoyed themed events but I was having a lot of trouble coming up with themes on my own. The names for the first few events that I hosted actually came from friends, for some reason my creativity seemed to be blocked. This was around the same time where I had really been getting deep in my activist research, spending up to 6 hours a day or more studying the things I have discussed in this book. It must have been very obvious to everyone around me that occult history and activism had pretty much consumed my interest, because many of my friends suggested that I themed my events around the things I was researching. The idea was brilliant and suddenly I no longer had any problem coming up with creative ideas for my shows. I did parties about sacred geometry, the Wall Street bailouts, free "end the fed" shows on tax day and many other events aimed at subtly educating the people who came out.

Eventually I was able to get a website set up thanks to the generosity of the raver who set up the domain and taught me the basics of the software. The website allowed me to host hundreds of educational activist documentaries and post independent news in an organized format on a daily basis. The website really took my research to a new level and eventually resulted in the book that you have just read.

I'm not the best writer in the world, I'm certainly not the best rave promoter and I'm not any smarter than your average person either. I have just spent my life confused about the social structure and why people behave the way they do, so I have continued to seek answers with every passing day. As time passed and I began to piece together more information I realized that most of what I was taught throughout my whole life was untrue. I had always suspected this but since I didn't have all of the information, I wasn't able to fully understand or specifically describe what I knew in my soul. I have always had a mentality that was in line with the principals of non-aggression and I was always aware that the major establishments in society didn't live up to those standards. For most of my life that vague idea was more or less the extent to my understanding of geo political and financial events. That all changed when I started researching things more thoroughly and came across the ideas and pieces of information that are contained in these pages.

Many synchronicities that I experienced during my adventures in the counter culture are eventually what led me to begin writing this book. I never had many resources or big time connections so when I began to think of new ways that I could contribute to the freedom movement, writing seemed like the only real option financially and logistically. Faster computers for video editing, music production software or podcasting equipment were not a financial possibility for me, but luckily writing doesn't cost anything. I knew that my path would be some form of art, because as I expressed many times I feel that human creativity is the only way to put an end to the violence and lack of compassion that is so prevalent in today's culture.

After I released my first book in 2011, I began writing articles for various alternative media sources. After about a year it became apparent that I had chosen a con artist as a publisher, causing me to become very discouraged with that path, so I began getting more involved in public activism. By

In 2013, I began taking on more public speaking appearances and became a daily writer for a number of websites. Prior to that I had only held seminars at the annual Big Dub Candy Mountain Festival, an outdoor rave event filled with many people that I would consider family. My first two speaking appearances in academic settings came in 2013, with appearances at the Free Your Mind Conference in Philadelphia and the Porcupine Freedom Festival in New Hampshire.

I also acted as a volunteer for all of these events, and eventually became one of the lead organizers for the Free Your Mind Conference. In 2014, Alchemy of the Timeless Renaissance, the book I had worked on for many years, is finally being released in an authorized form. Now I am working on writing more books, putting together events like the raves that I host with Good Vibes Promotions, and also organizing academic events like the Free Your Mind Conference.

Our Journeys: About the Authors:

Derrick Broze

In my short 30 years on this planet I have been a child, a musician, a convict, a promoter, a liar, an activist, a gardener, a spiritual being, journalist and so much more. The last few years of my life I have made major efforts to heal and merge all these aspects of myself into one balanced human. It is not always an easy task but I believe this book will be an important part of that effort.

Since 2011 I have been pulled further into the direction of self-exploration and activism. Most of my experience with activism, and specifically Anarchy, has been through underground book stores, and infoshops. These community centers embodied the spirit of mutual aid and breaking down false barriers. Over time I learned that my politics did not agree with many of those who were a part of this culture but I always loved the communal, non-oppressive environment. This experience helped shaped my views and understanding of Left Anarchist politics. Without those lessons I do not think I would have come to understand Anarchy as I do now.

While I was examining my physical world and working to better understand the nature of government, I was also beginning to better know my internal world. Since I have already mentioned my time behind bars and traveling on the road I will leave those details out. Needless to say those experiences shaped my outlook greatly. Without these experiences I do not believe I would have been able to get at the root causes of my pain and begin the ever-important process of healing.

It was also my time as a provider of LSD that I first began to question the nature of reality and to push the boundaries of my belief systems. Later I would discover meditation which would set the stage for my spiritual pursuits.

By 2012 I had decided that I could no longer work for "The Man" and would rather be poor (or even homeless) if it meant I could be happy and free. Thankfully my activism began to get noticed in Houston and around the globe and in the Spring of 2013 John Vibes helped me get my first writing job. Since that time my work and network has increased and as of the printing of this book I am writing for 4 different publications, in addition to my still ongoing community activism in Houston.

My path towards Panarchy and Spiritual Awareness was equally shaped by my time as a promoter of music and art events. In 2009 I started a booking collective called Visionary Noise. Since that time I have worked with a partner to turn VN into one of the most recognized names in promotion in the Houston area. Through promoting events and local shows I have come to understand that any sustainable movement aiming to create change must be rooted in the community. We cannot just promote ideas related to economics and philosophy but we must strive to engage the artist communities to help foster a new culture that reflects our values.

Equally important has been my time as a gardener. My 2011 bike tour gave me an opportunity to spend time on farms to witness firsthand the power and beauty of a self-sufficient lifestyle. Upon returning from my bike tour I started my own gardening business, Organic Gardens For All, and have worked to bring the people of Houston closer to the ideas of home and community gardens. I have learned so much through my time in the soil and Sun.

Now here I am in 2015: a journalist; an activist; a gardener; a spiritual student; musician; promoter; and who knows what else is next! In the immediate future I plan to promote the ideas contained within these pages as well as move further into living the Agorist principles and lifestyle.

Thank you for reading our book! See you out there in the Free World!

Acknowledgements

Derrick Broze

This book would not have been possible without the many amazing, supportive people I have been blessed to meet on my path. There are far too many to name them all so I apologize ahead of time if you do not see your name here.

First off, Thank You to the Great Spirit that moves in all life. Thank you to my family for always being supportive. Thank you to Be Amor for constant love, companionship, and encouragement. Without you I could not have made this journey.

A special thanks to Micah Jackson for valuable insight and education on philosophy.

A big thanks to The Conscious Resistance Network team: Damon Shaw, Danilo Cuellar, Katy DeFazio, Francis Ysdoras, Brandon BC, Tryp, Jeffer Thomasson, Anthony Aguero, Sam Wagner, Michael King, and of course Neil Radimaker.

And in no particular order thank you to the following people for inspiration and strength: Adam Kokesh, Ben Swann, John Bush, Catherine Bleish, Danny Panzella, Huang Po, John Trudell, Samuel E. Konkin III,

Joe Martino of Collective-Evolution.com, Ernesto Jara, Jade The Creator, Oskar Yetzirah, Joe Medina, Paul Osman, Cody Adams, Colin Staffieri, my brothers in MANINKARI, Dillon Loftus, Edgar Amador, Britney Miranda, Jacquelyn Samperi, Richard Dee, Joe Zenner, Randa Fox, Hailey Spates, Alex Fischer, and Rosie Soto. Thank you to all the Houston Free Thinkers and my spiritual family for holding it down in H-Town.

And lastly, thank you to my brother John Vibes for joining me on this important piece of work and all of the financial contributors who made this project a reality.

Acknowledgements

John Vibes

This list will be short because I have had so many great people help me along my path that I don't want to risk leaving any of them out.

However, I would like to give a special thanks to the sites that I currently write for, thefreethoughtproject.com, trueactivist.com, theantimedia.org, punkrocklibertarians.com, notbeinggoverned.com, as well as the sites that gave me my start, activistpost.com and intellihub.com.

I would also like to thank Mark Passio for his confidence in entrusting me with the Free Your Mind Conference and Bob Tuskin for giving me my first radio interview.

None of this would be accomplished if it was not for my wife and family, so I am eternally grateful for their support and guidance.

And lastly, thank you to my brother Derrick Broze for joining me on this important piece of work and all of the financial contributors who made this project a reality.

To find out more about The Conscious Resistance and to order more books please visit: theconsciousresistance.com/book